Dedicated to all young explorers and artists.
Let your imagination roar with excitement as you
embark on colorful adventures.

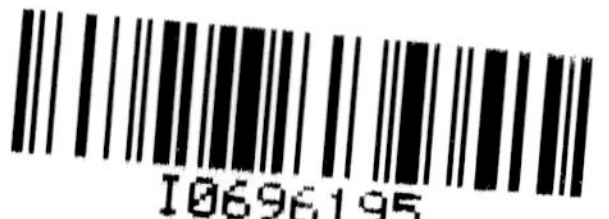

AWS

01/2024

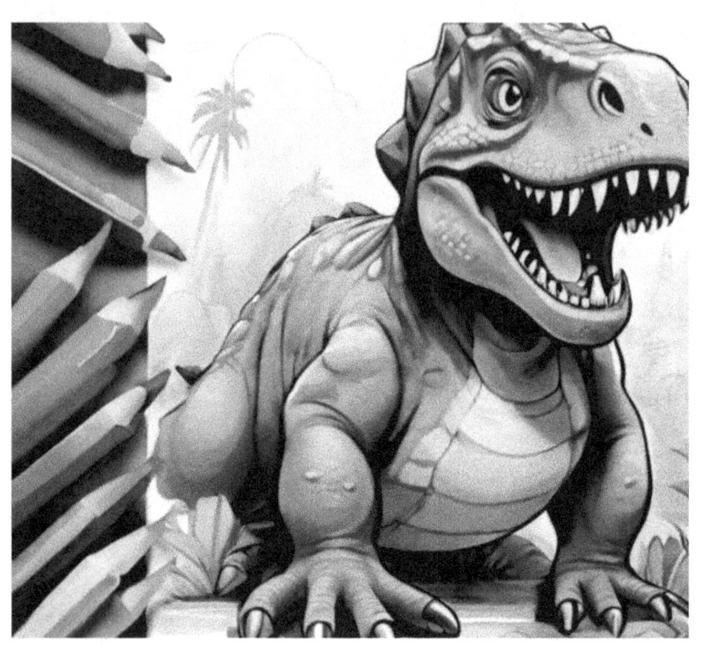
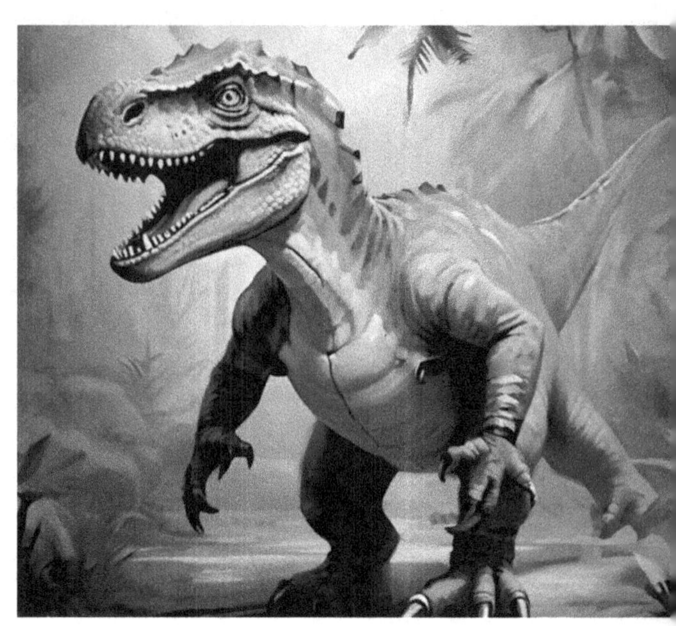

THE BOOK BELONGS TO:

____

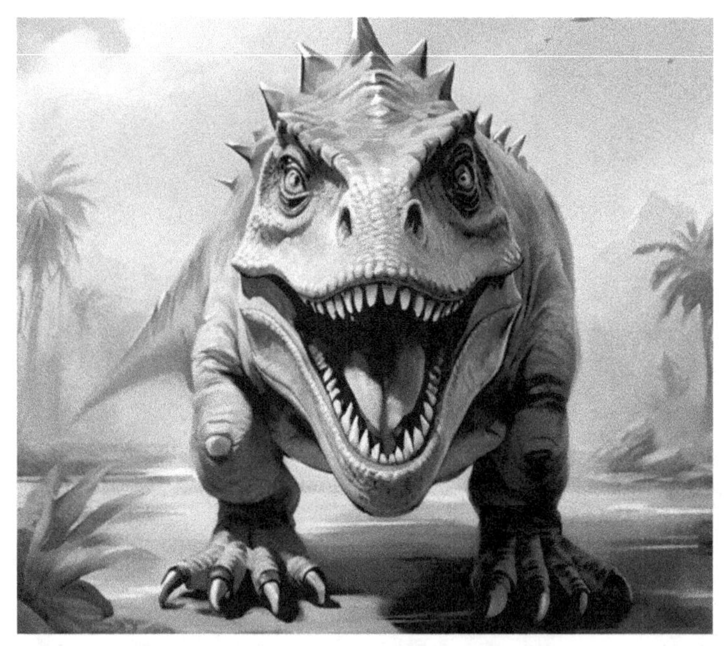
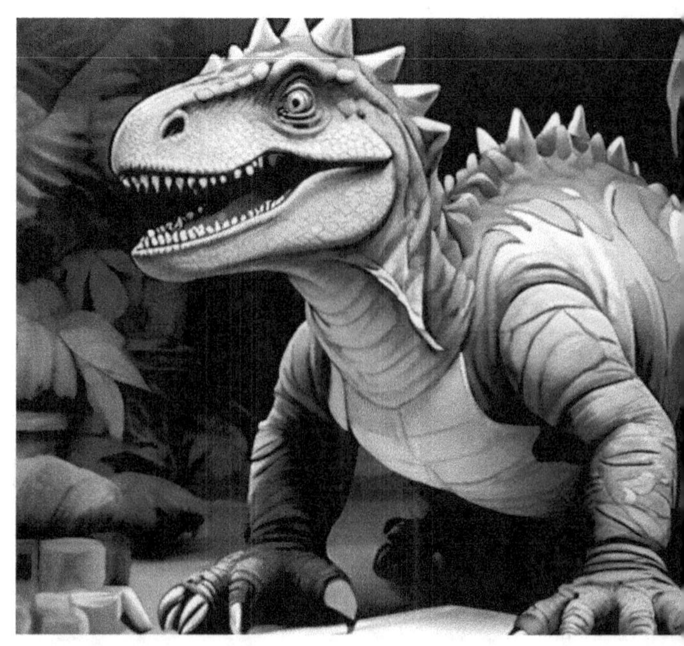

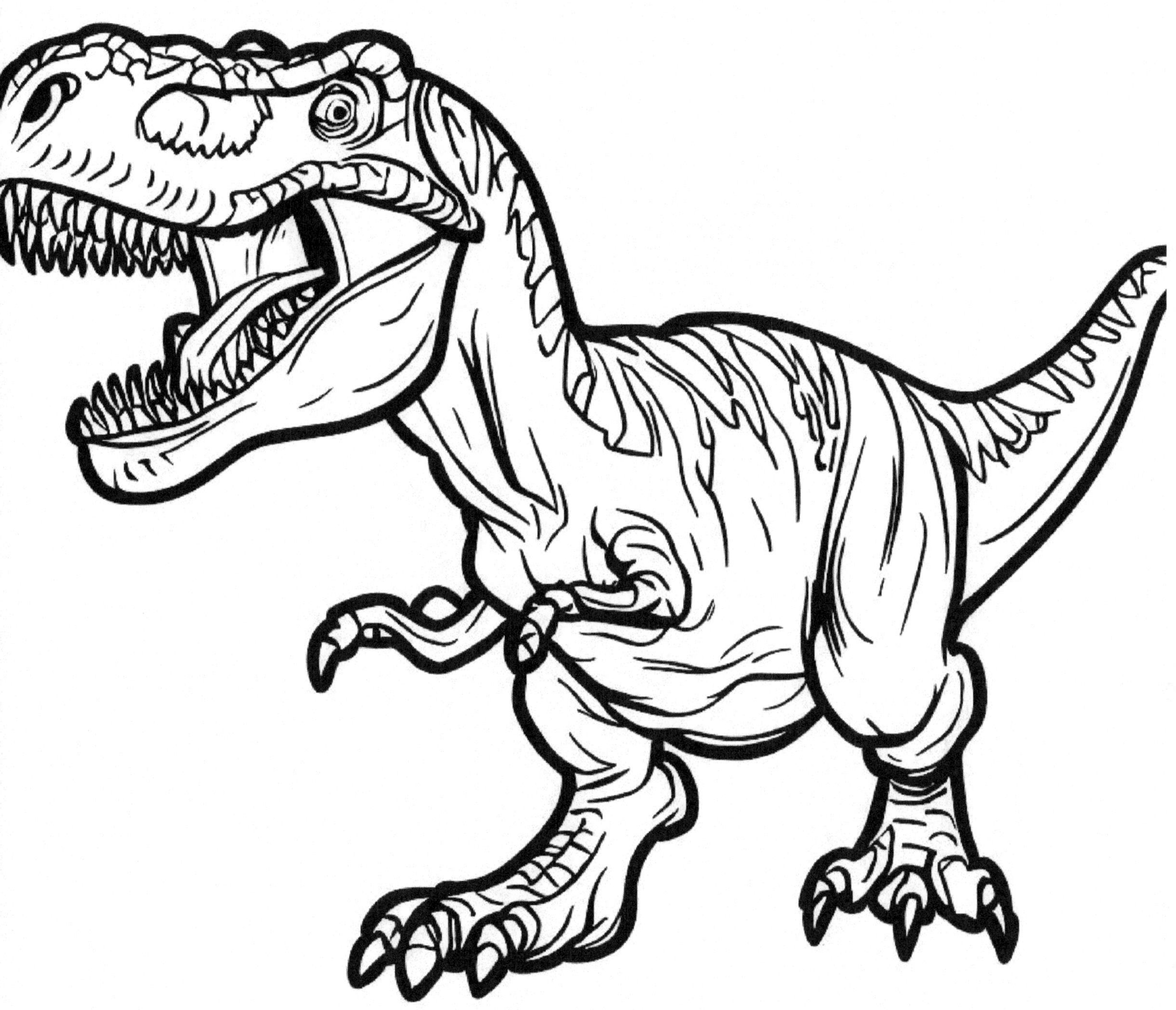

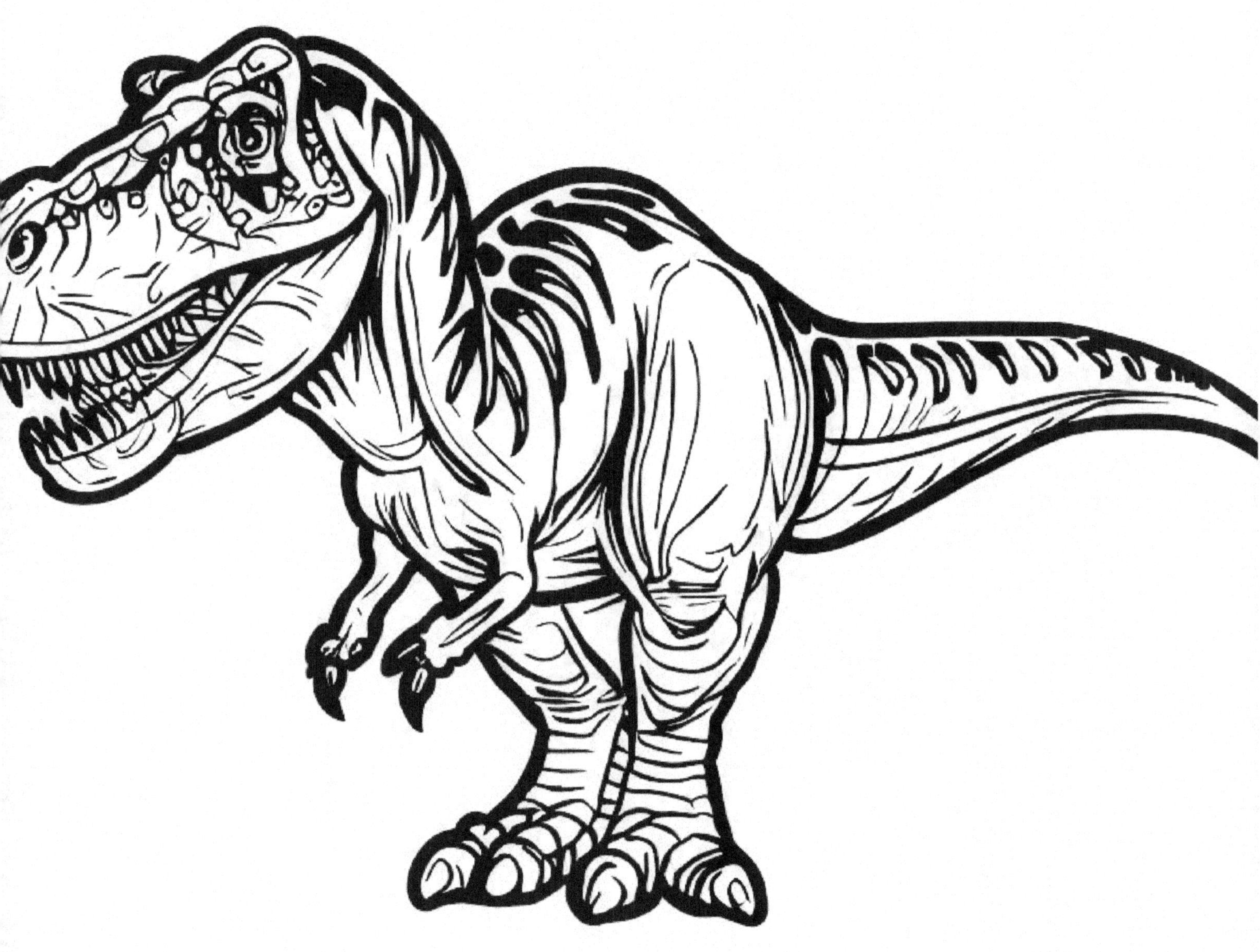

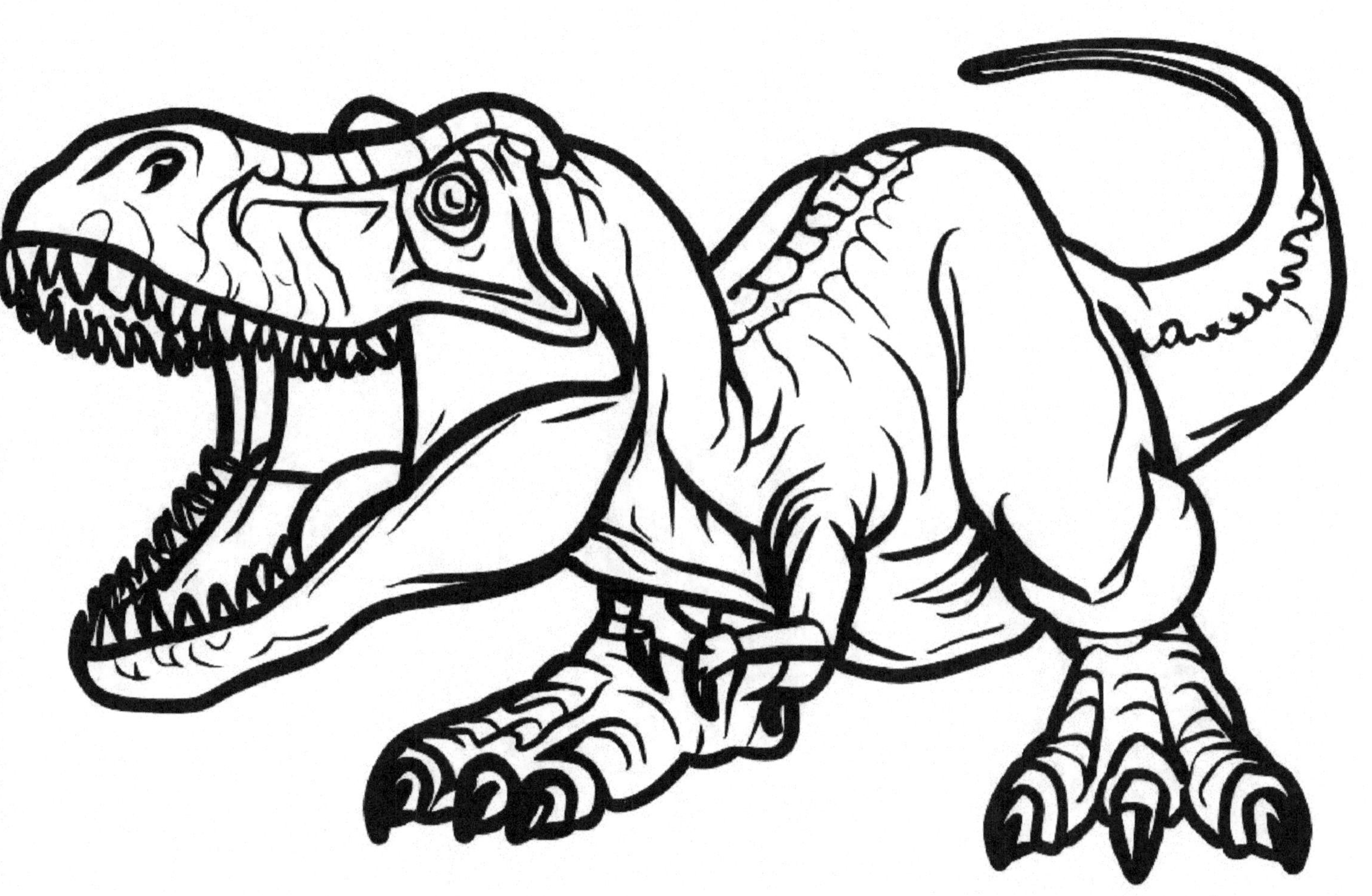

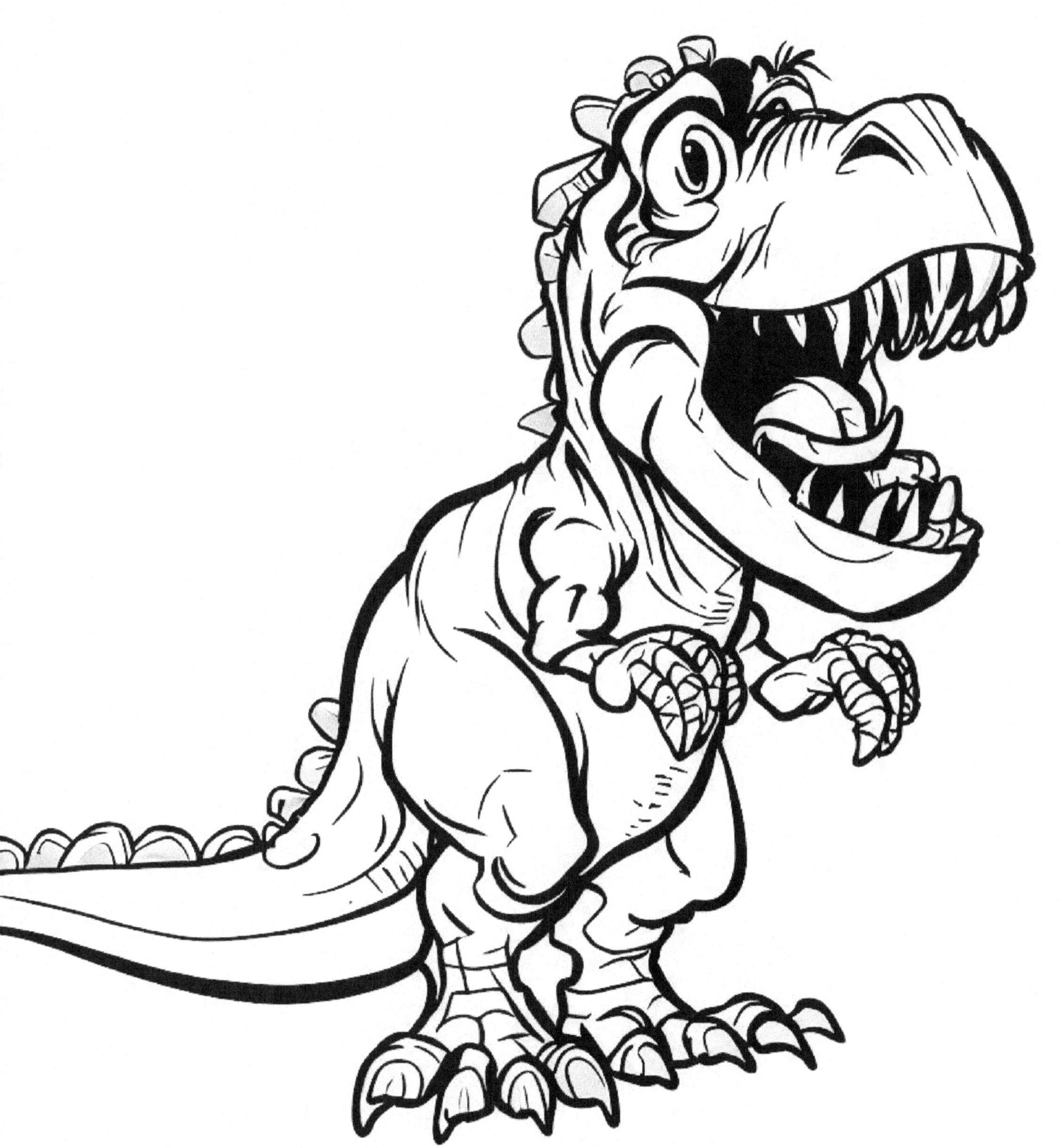

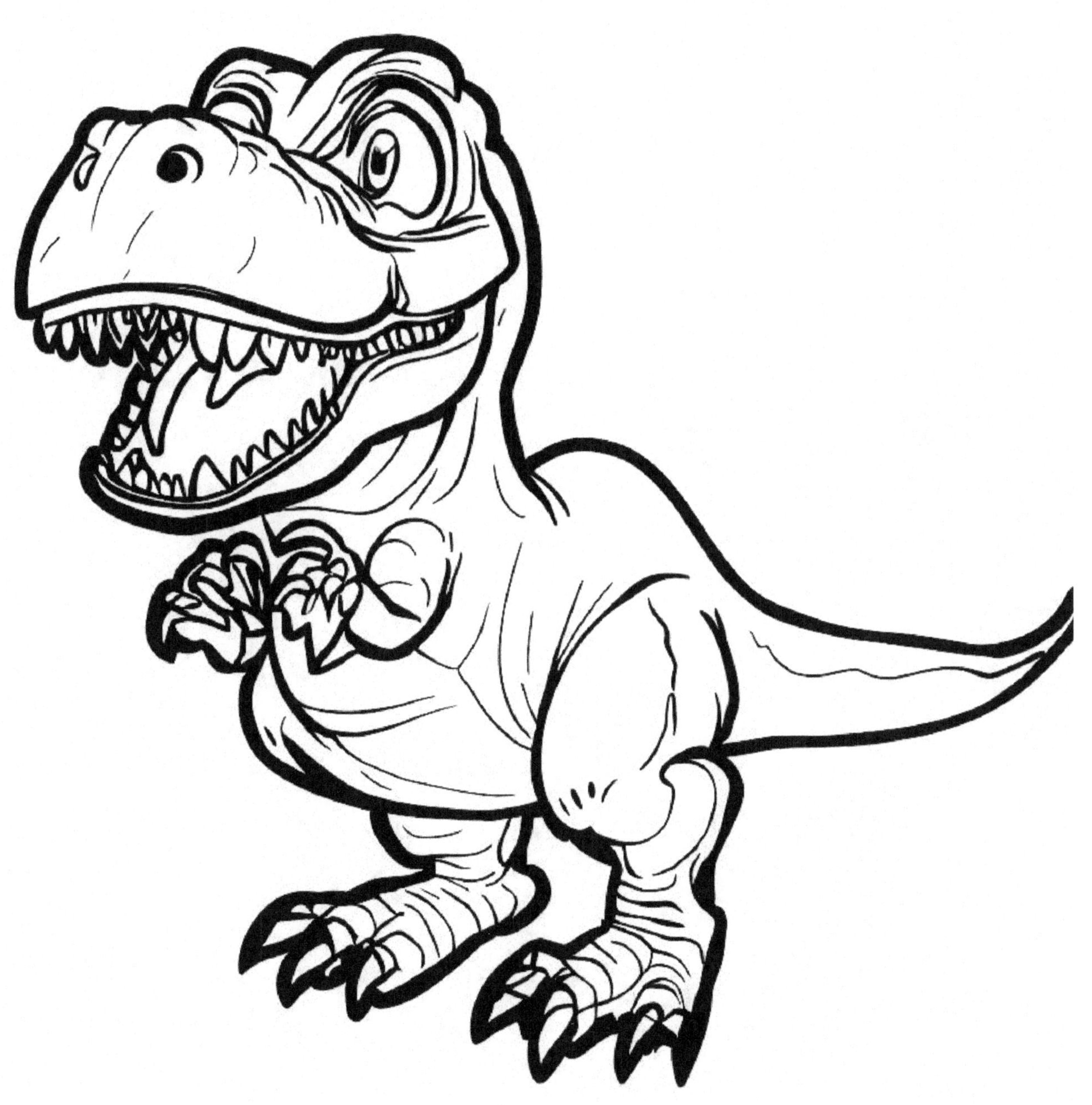

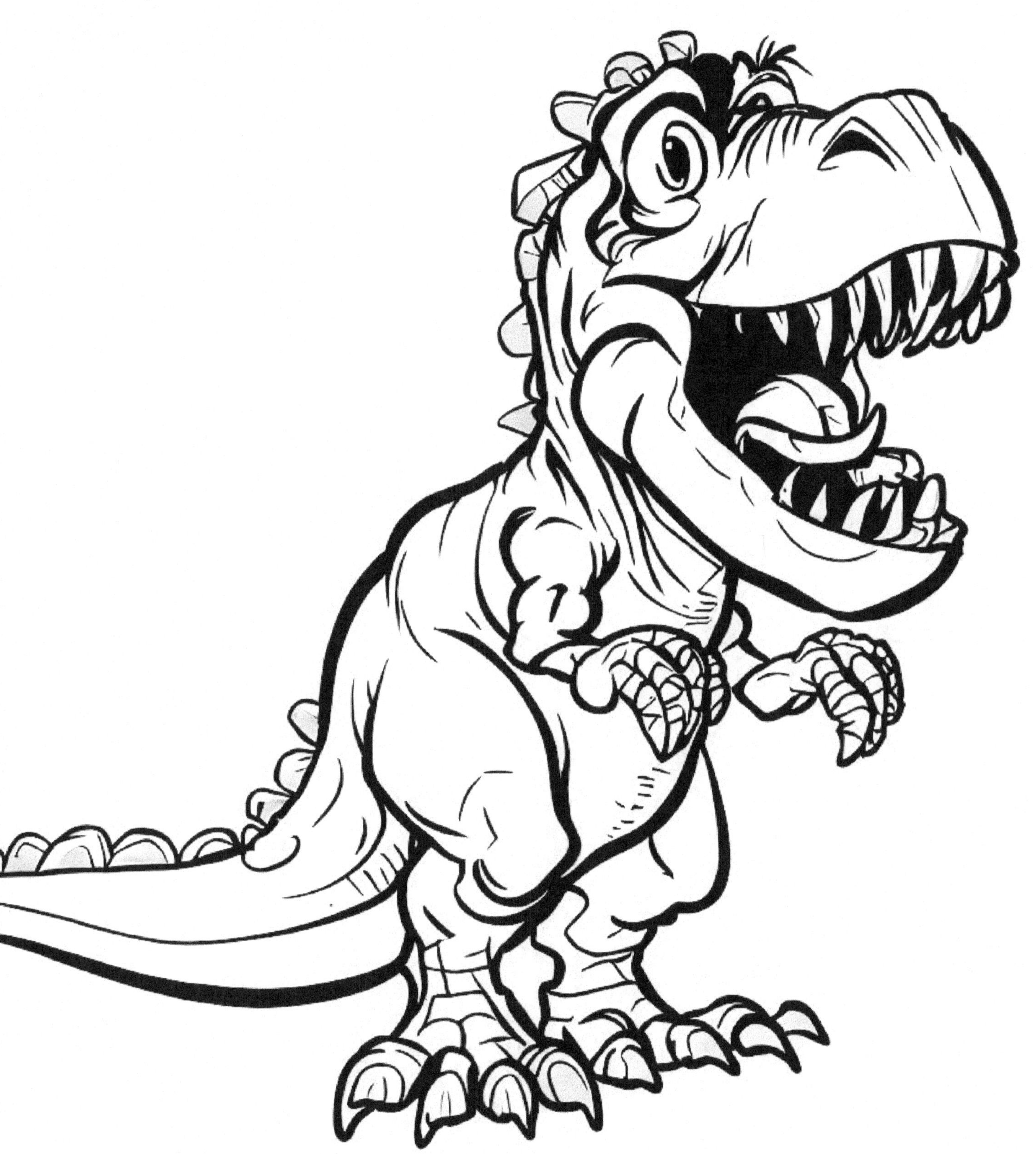

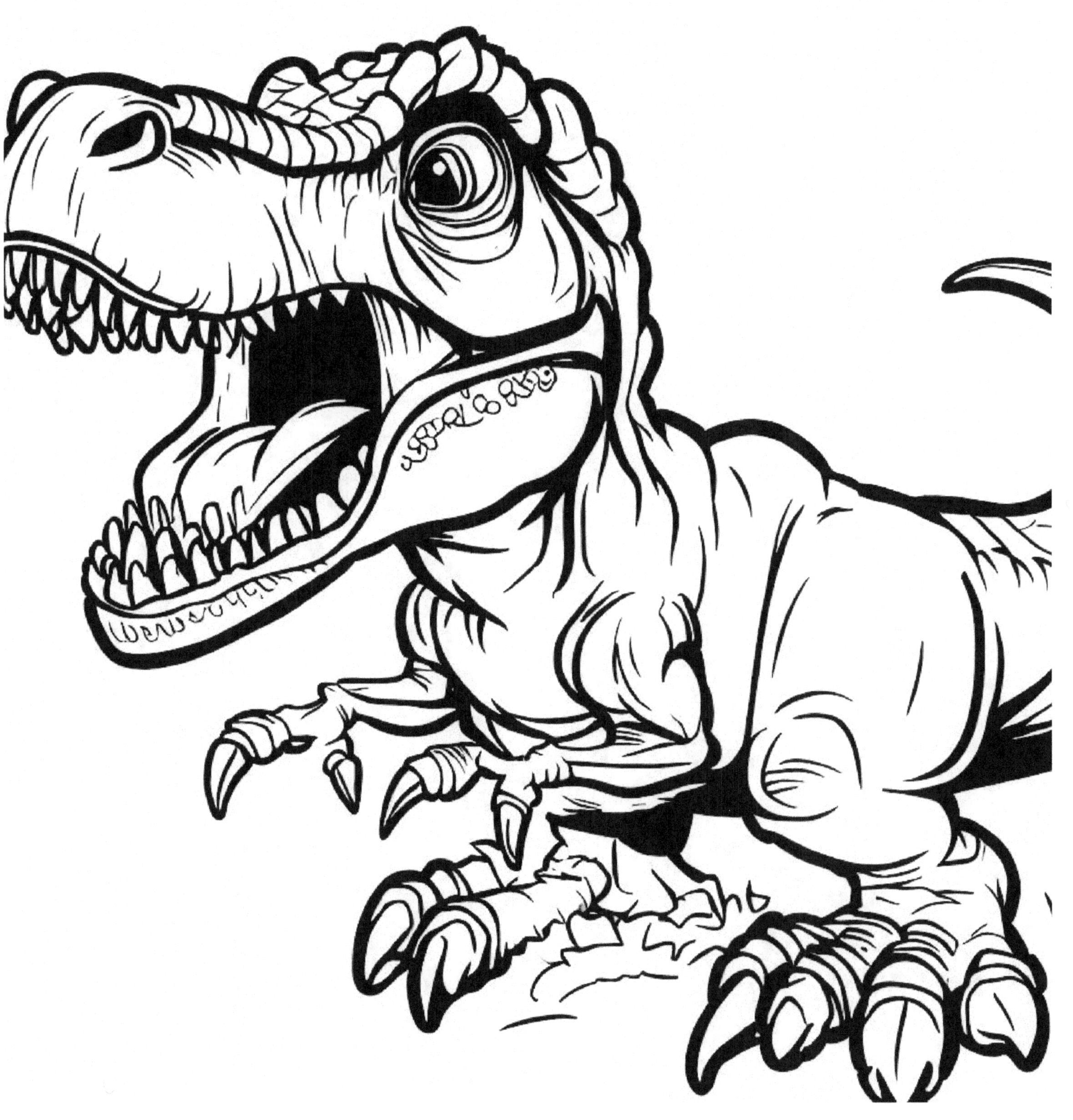

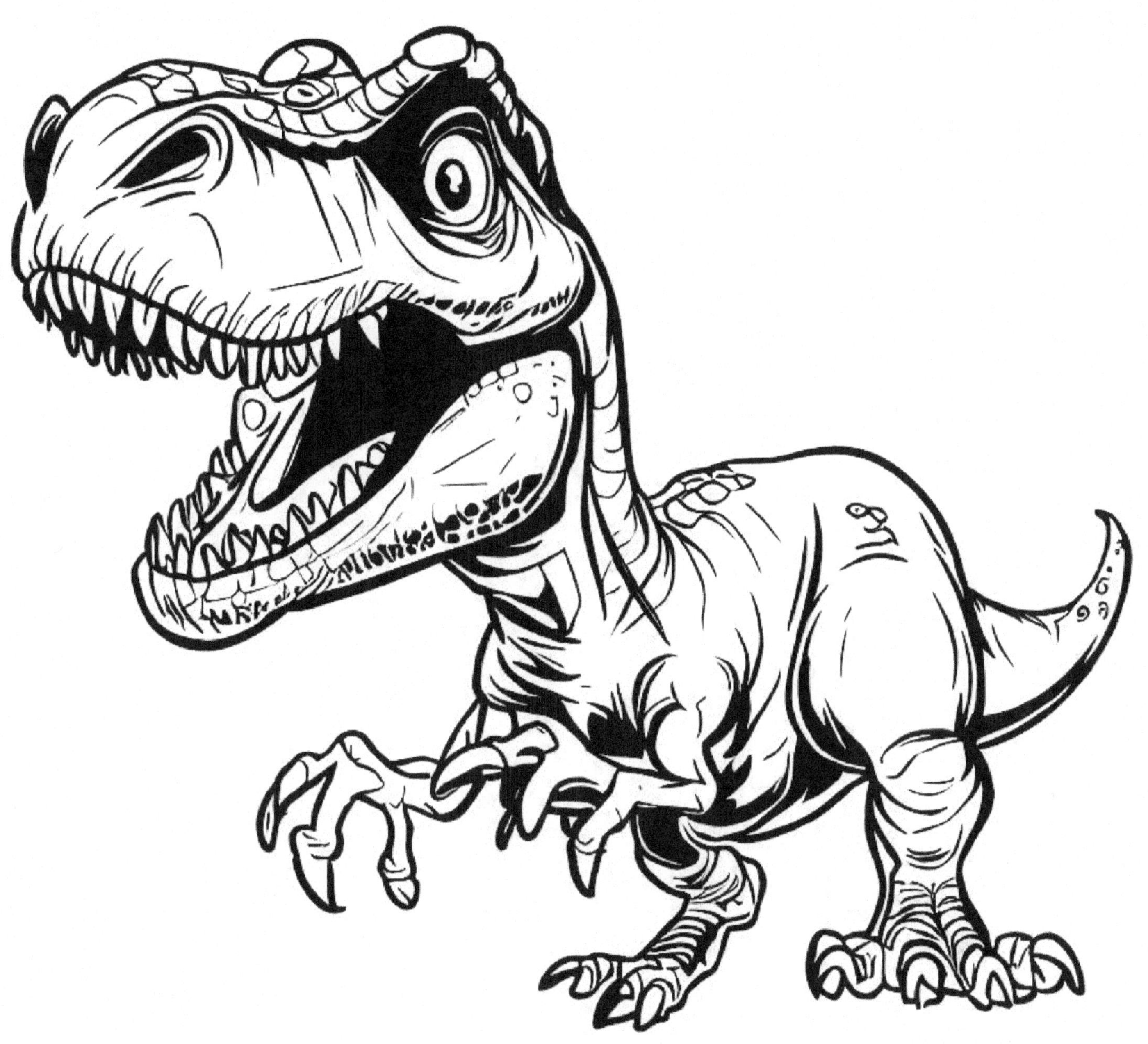

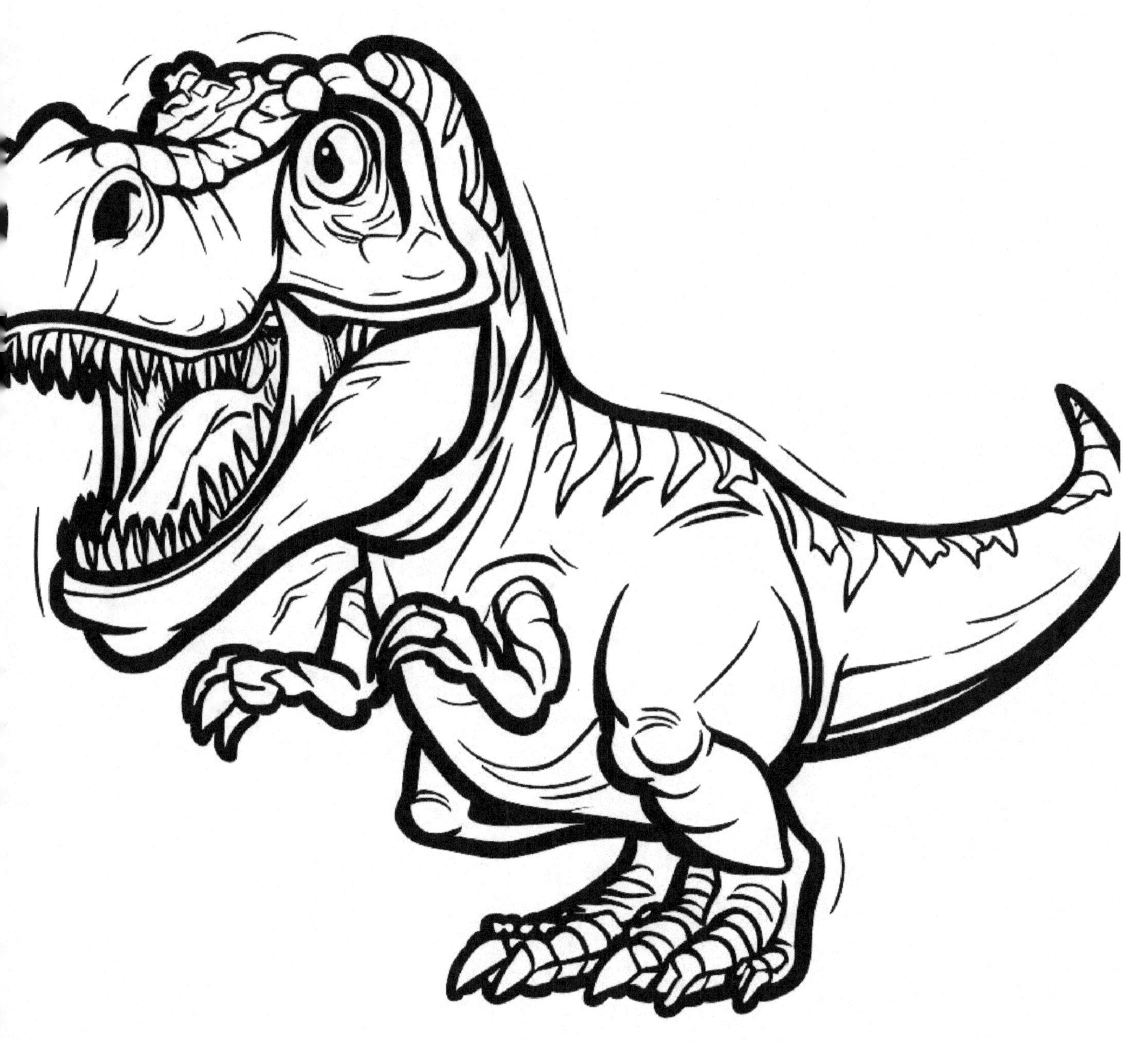

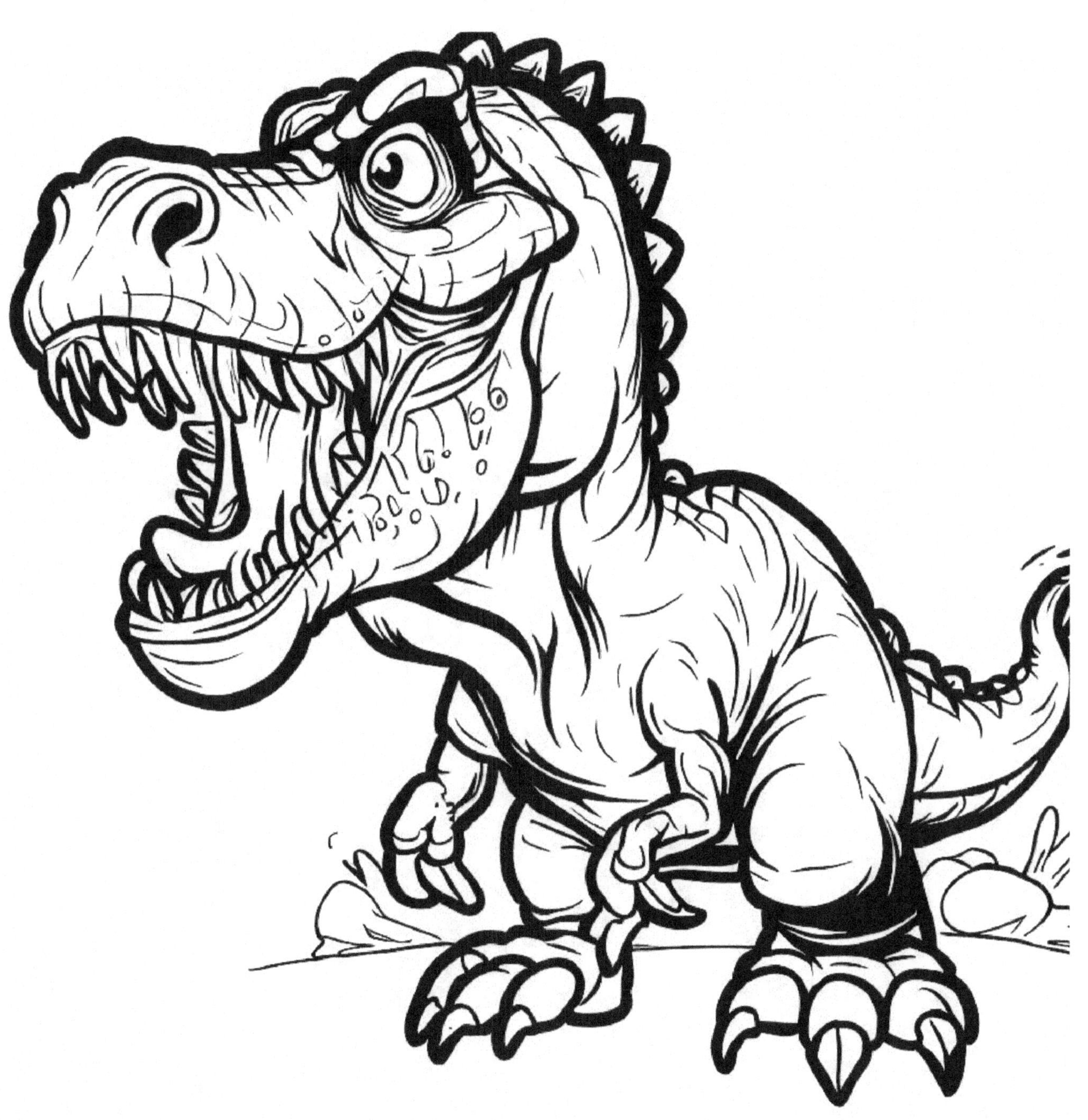

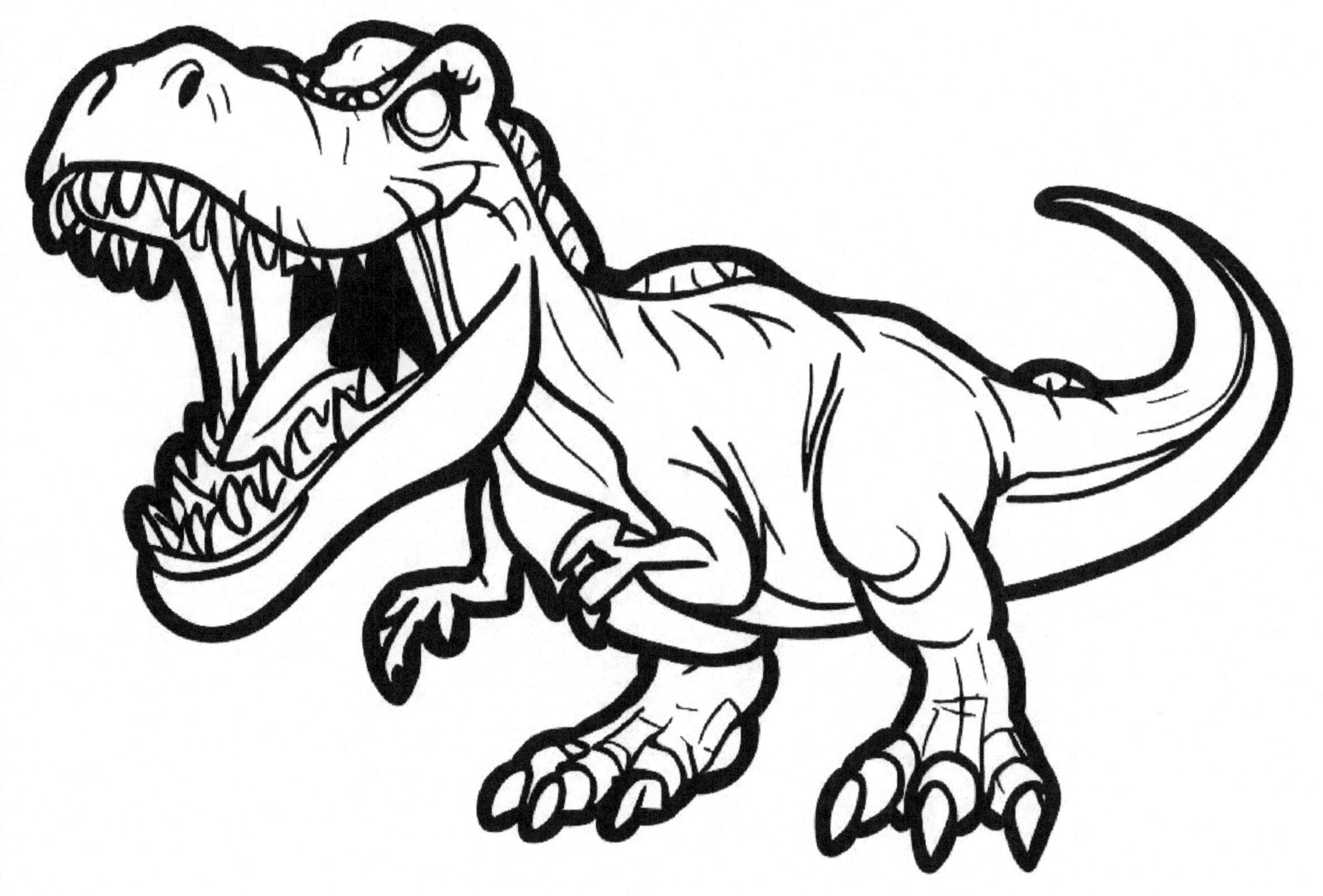

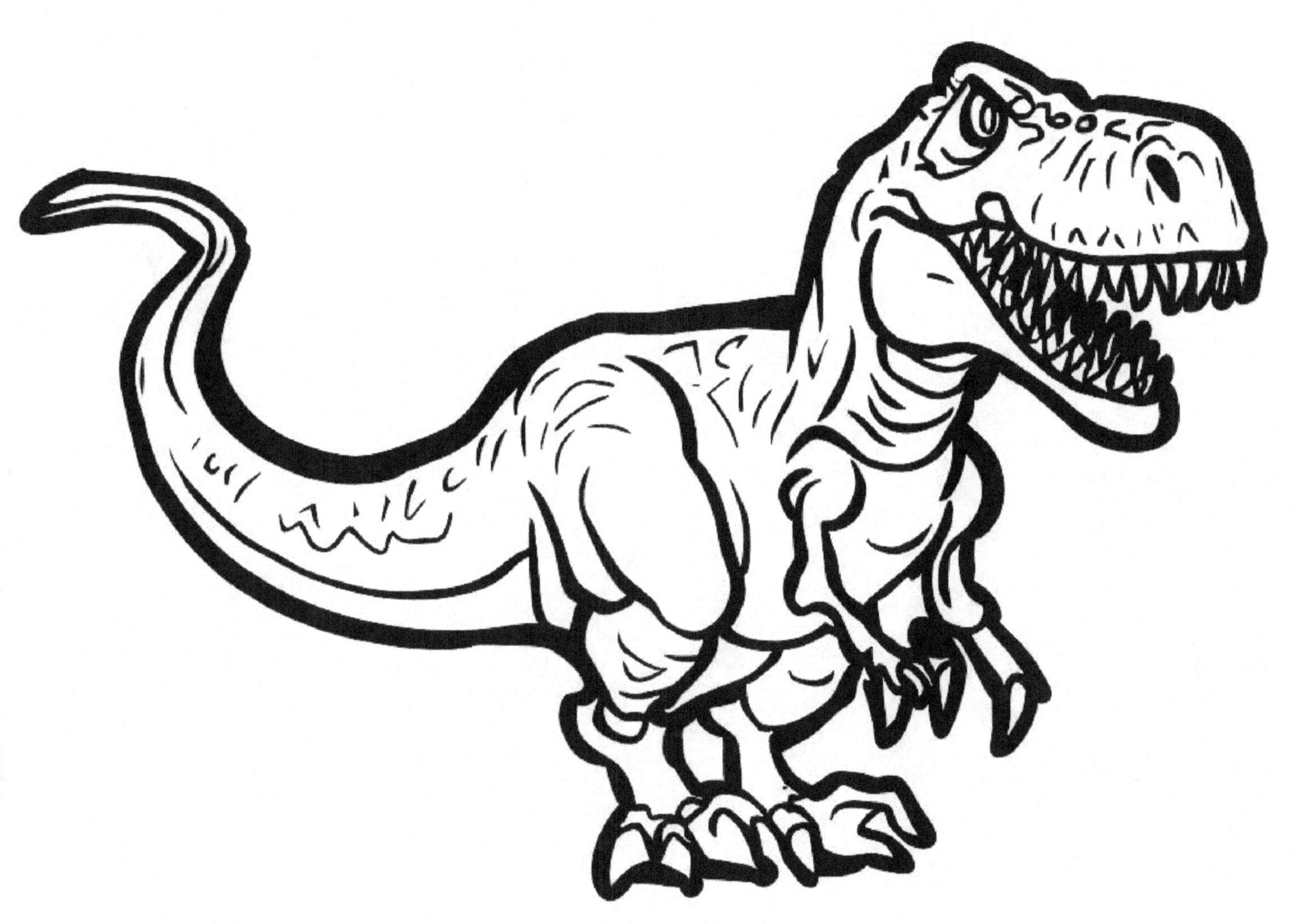

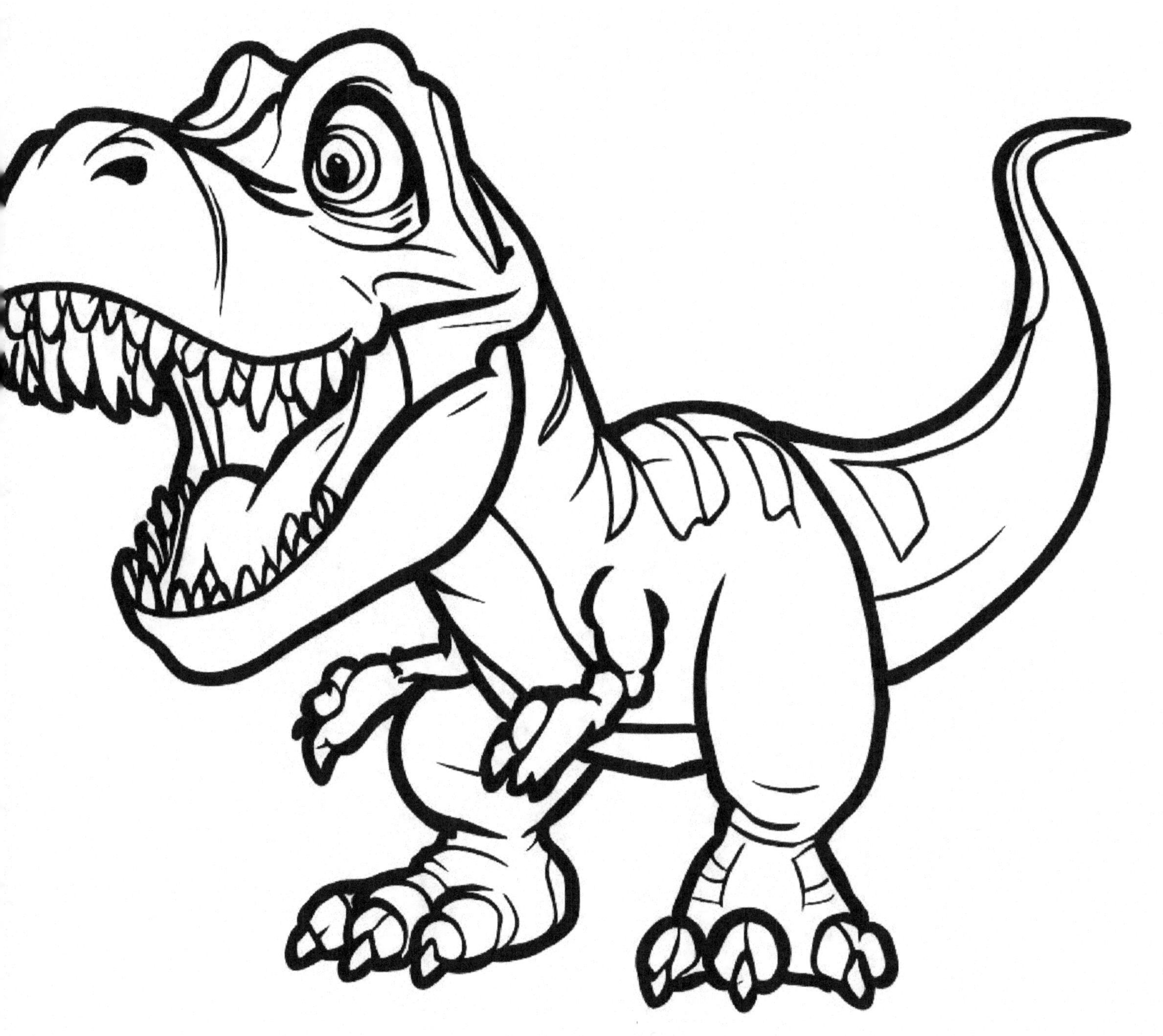

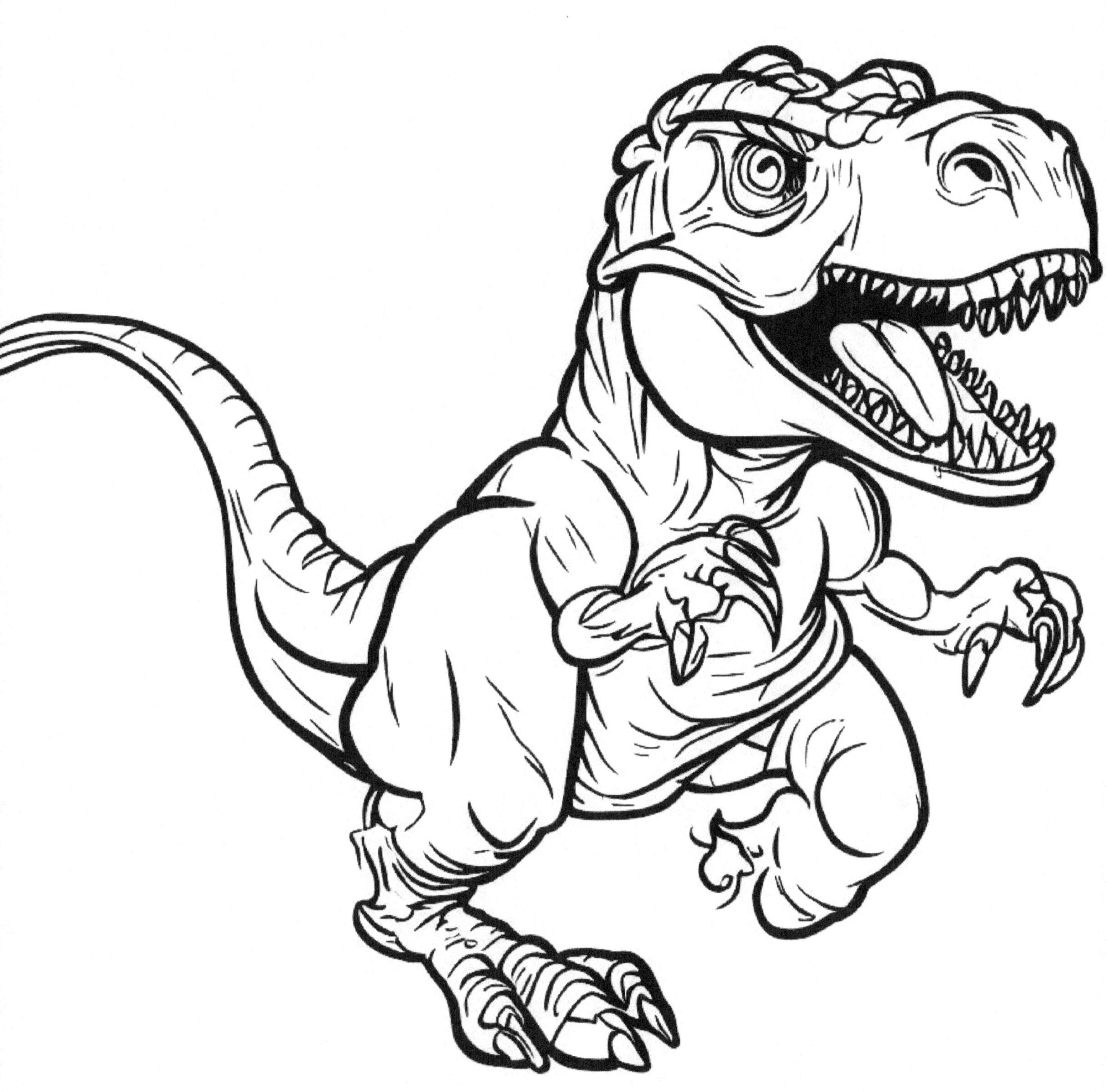

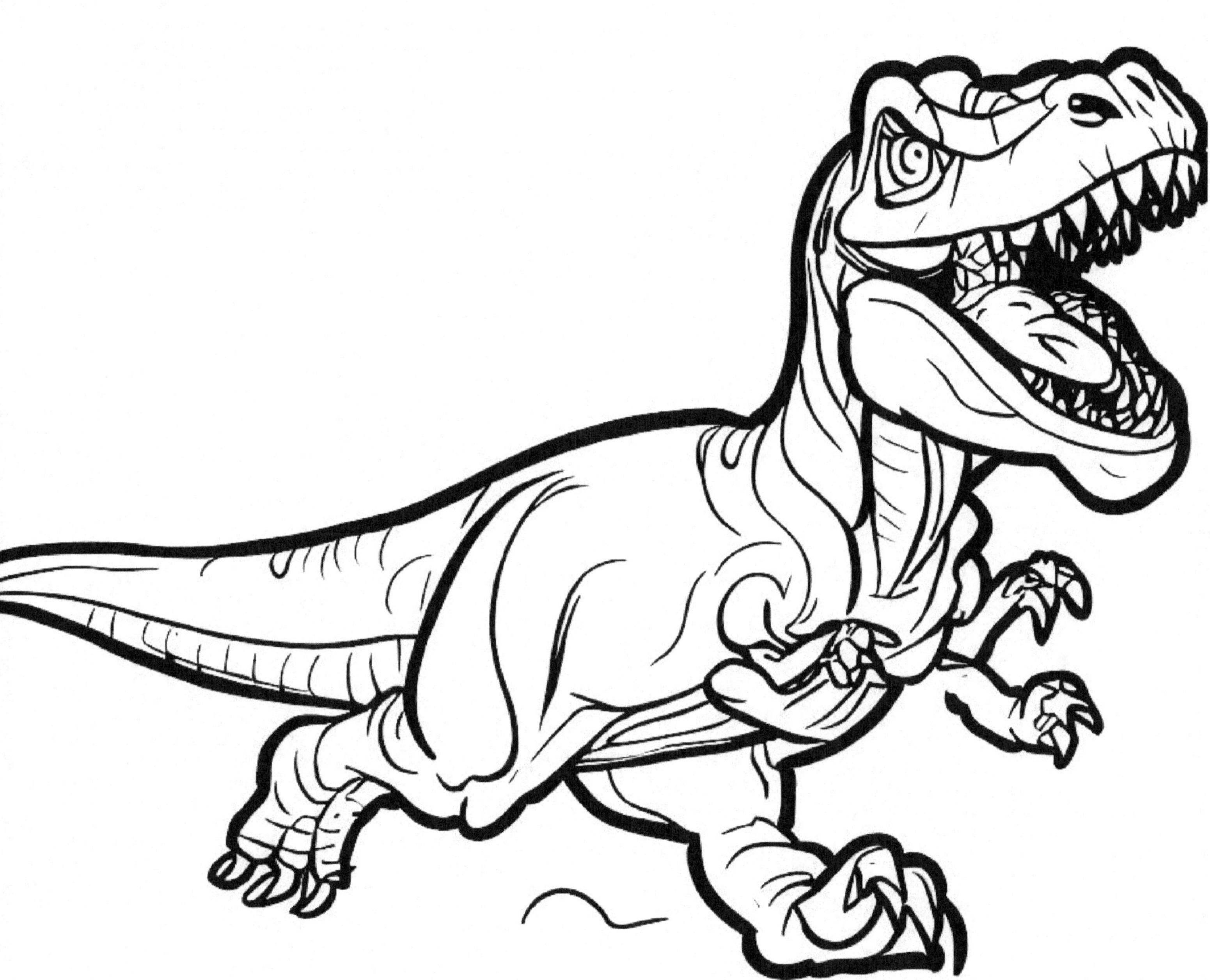

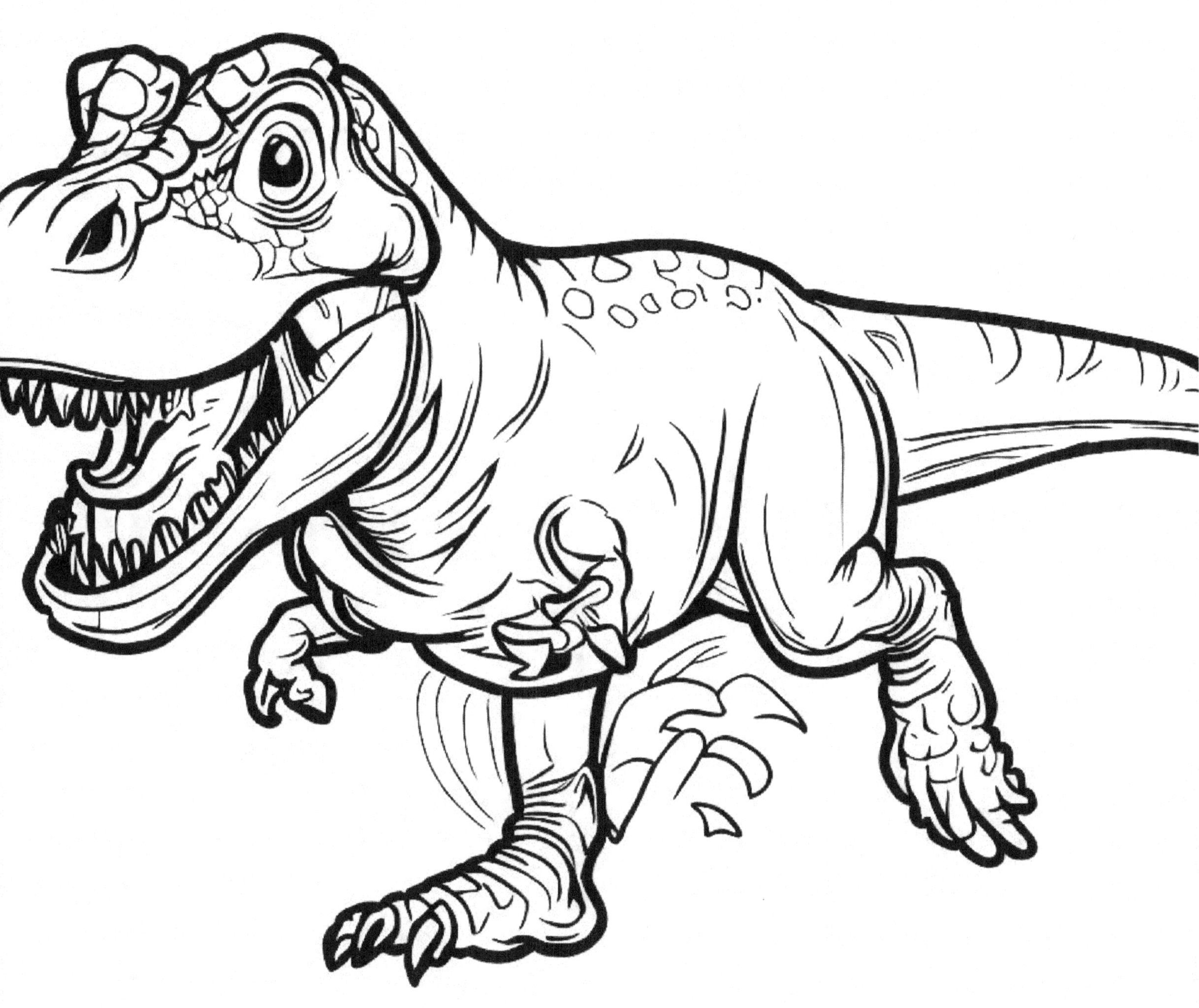

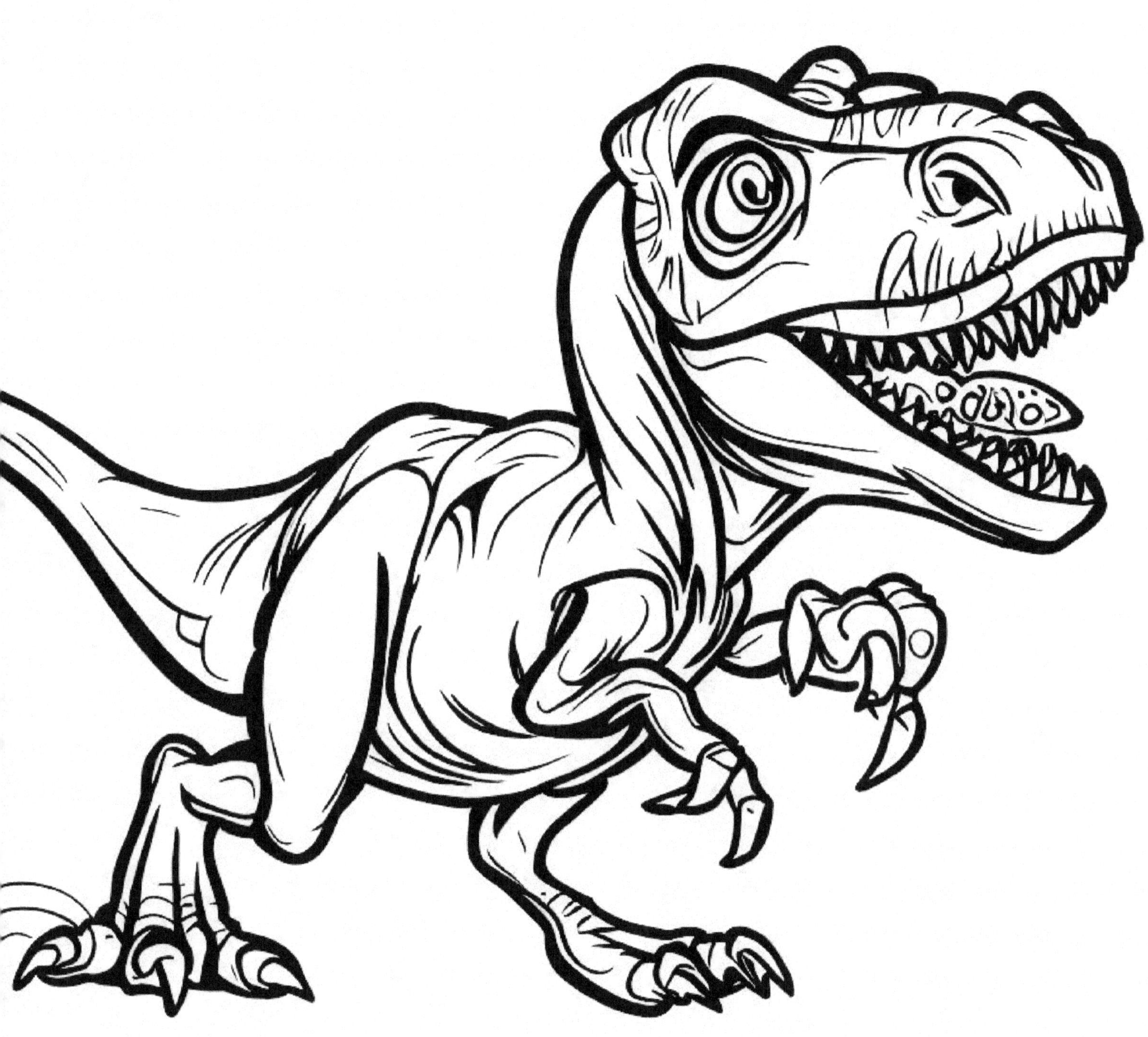

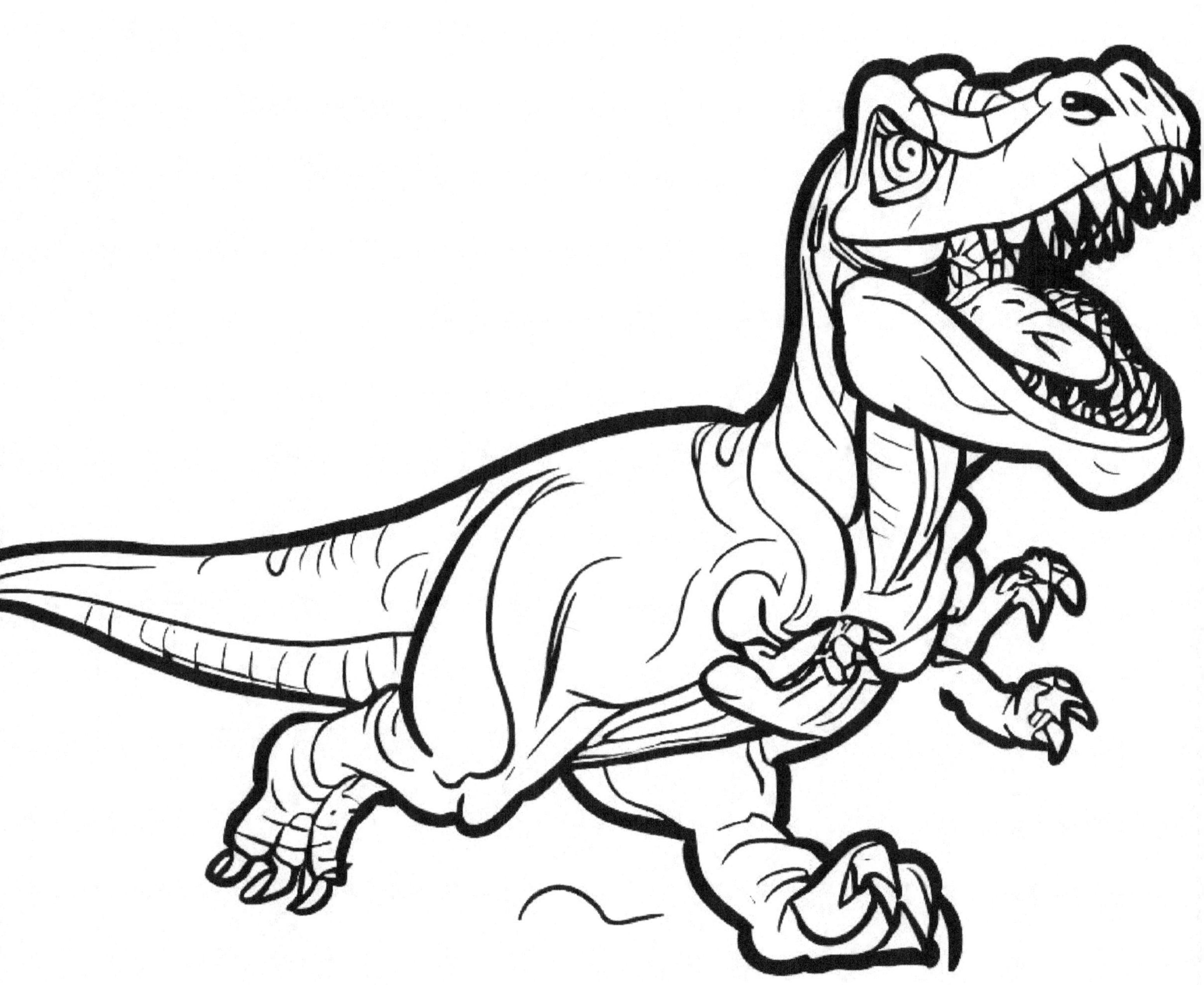

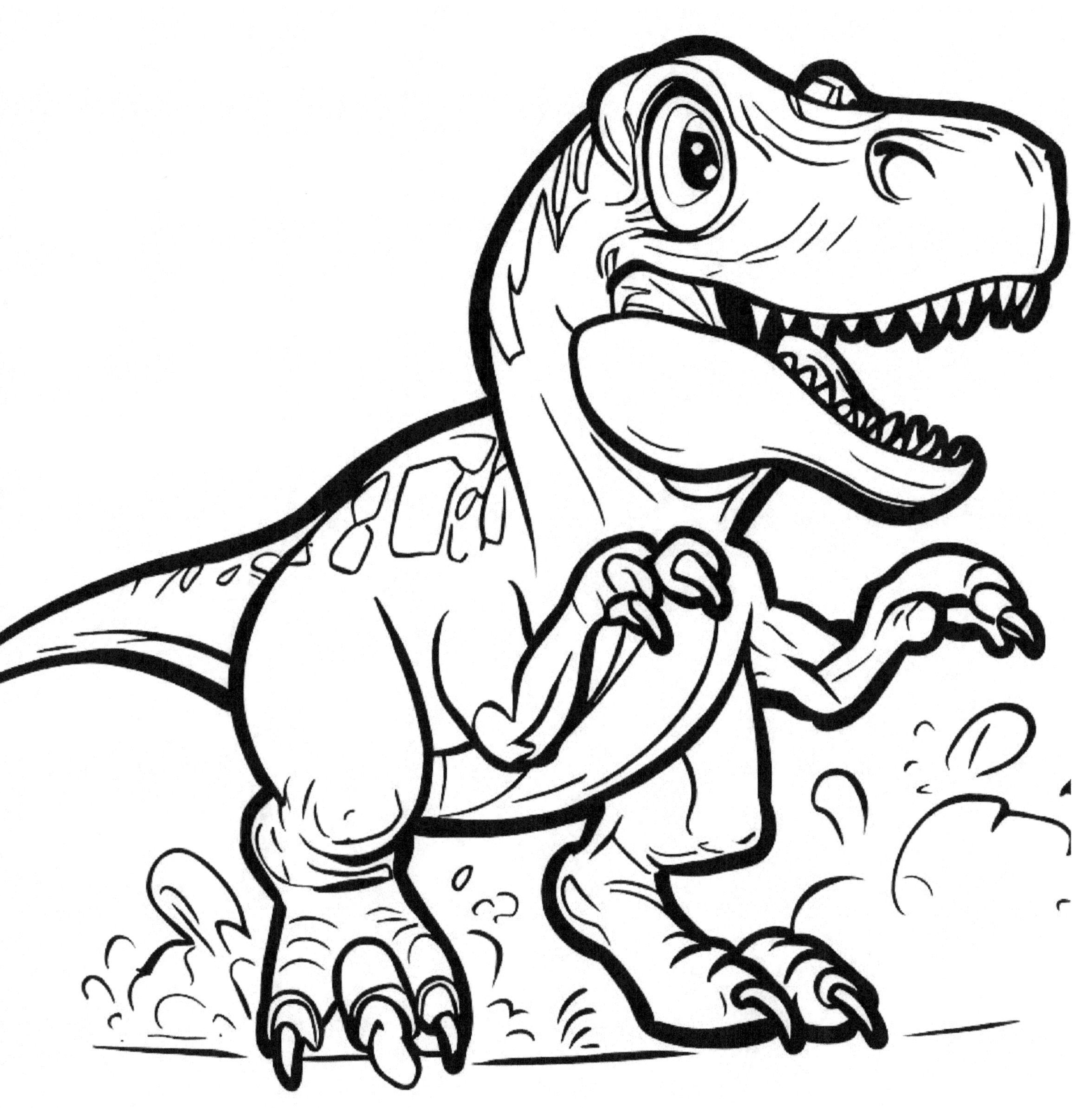

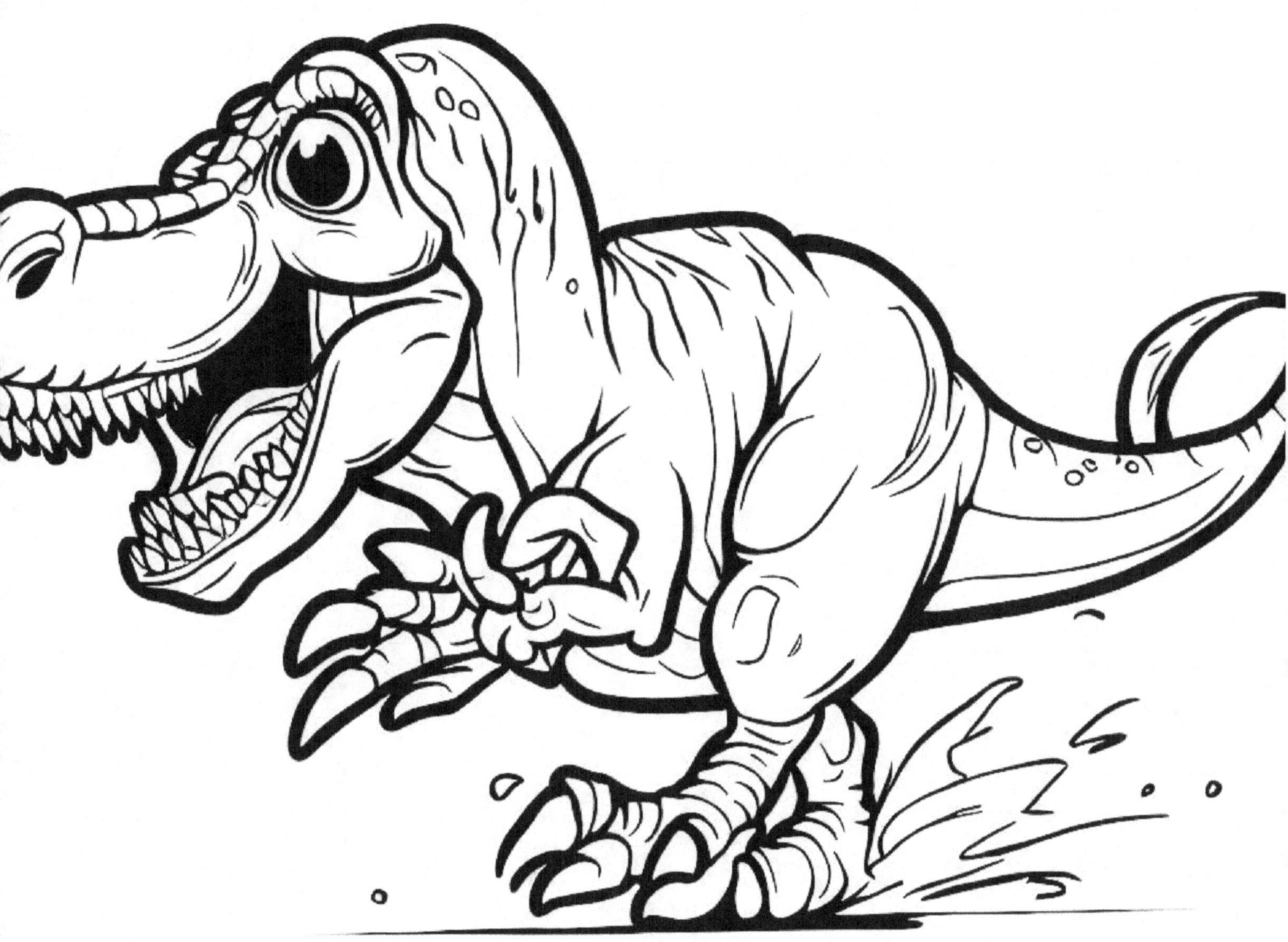

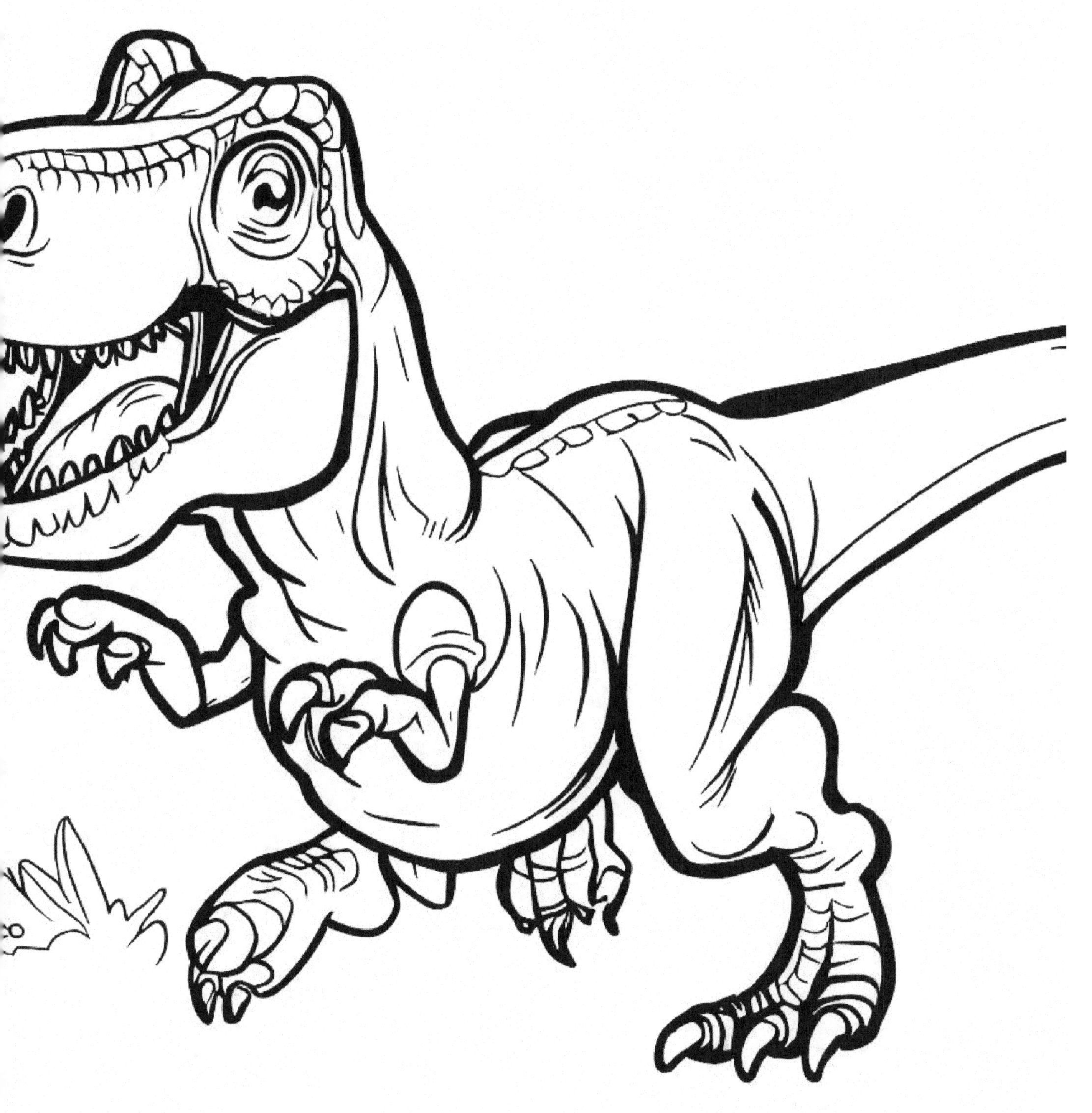

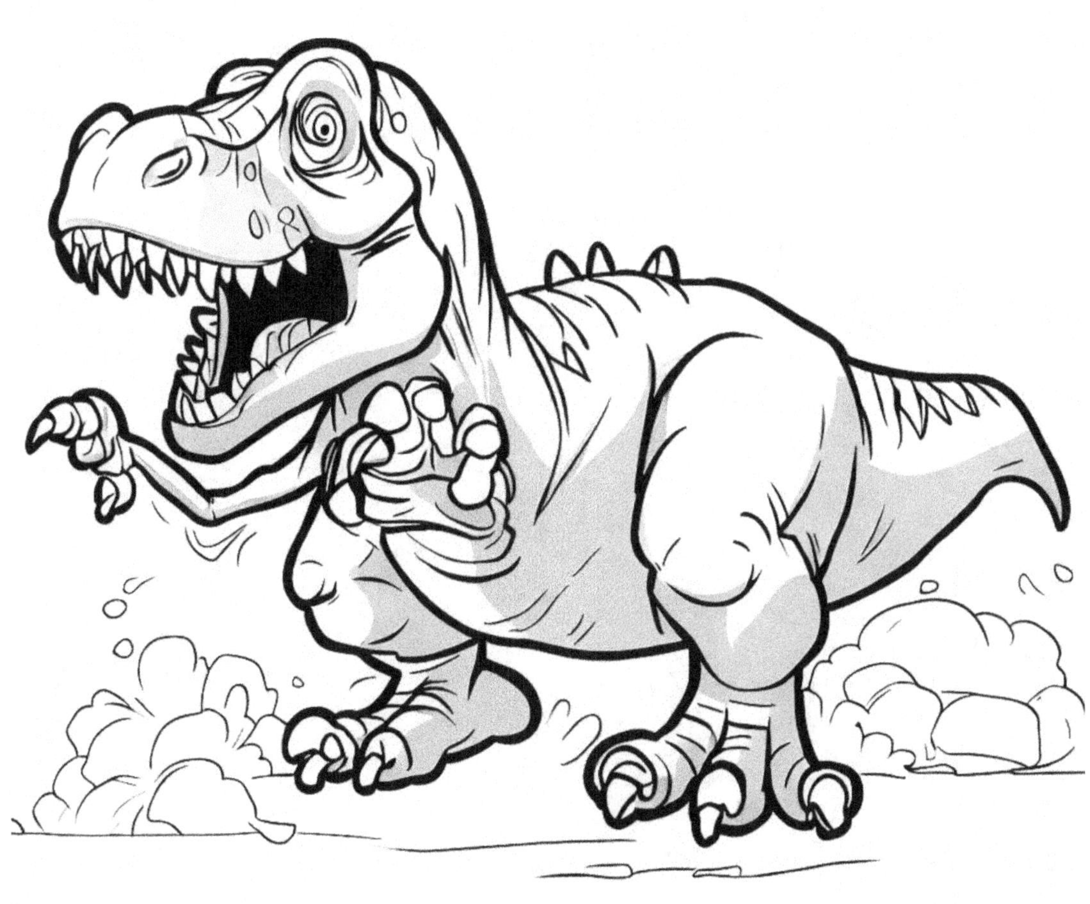

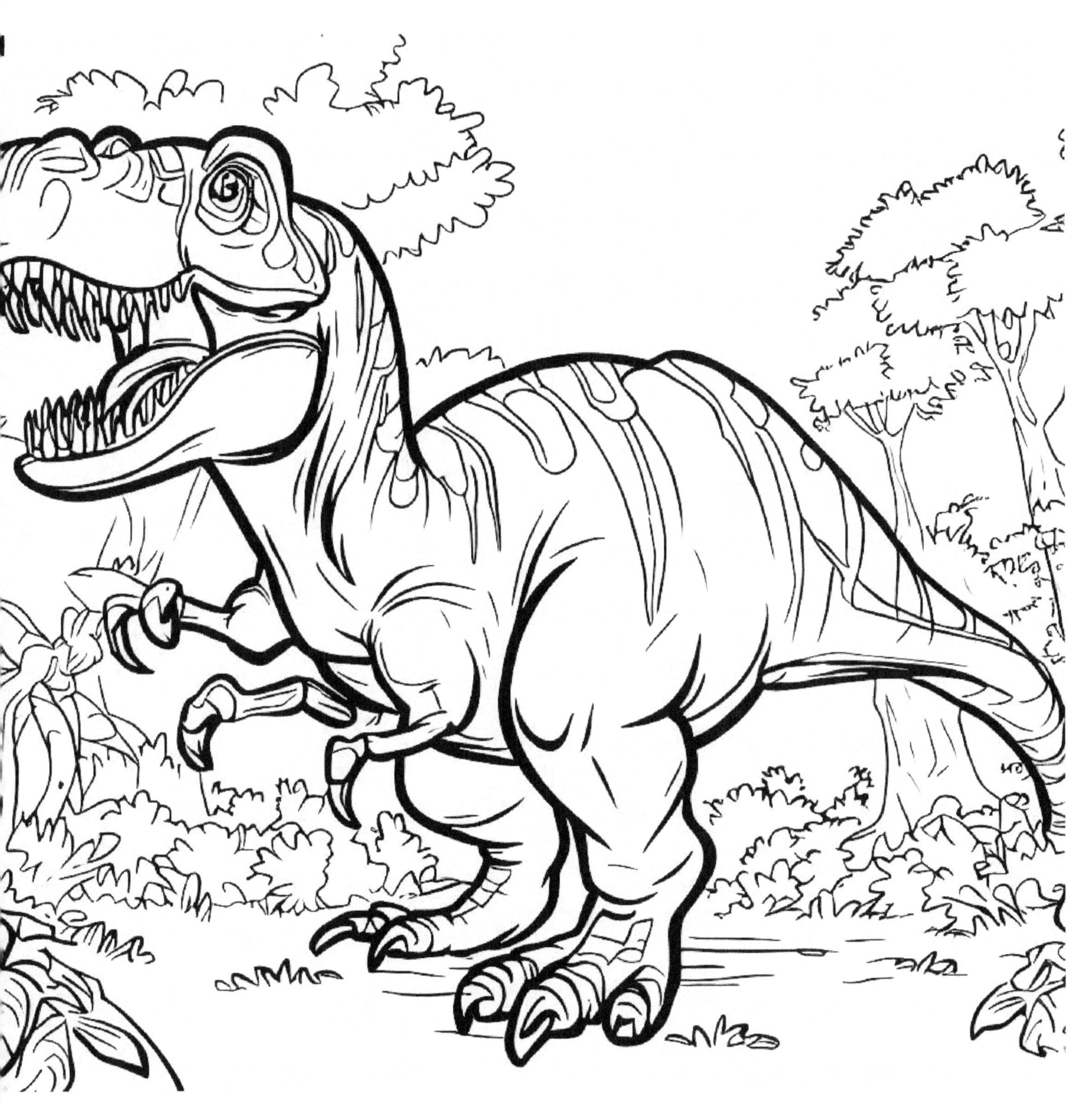

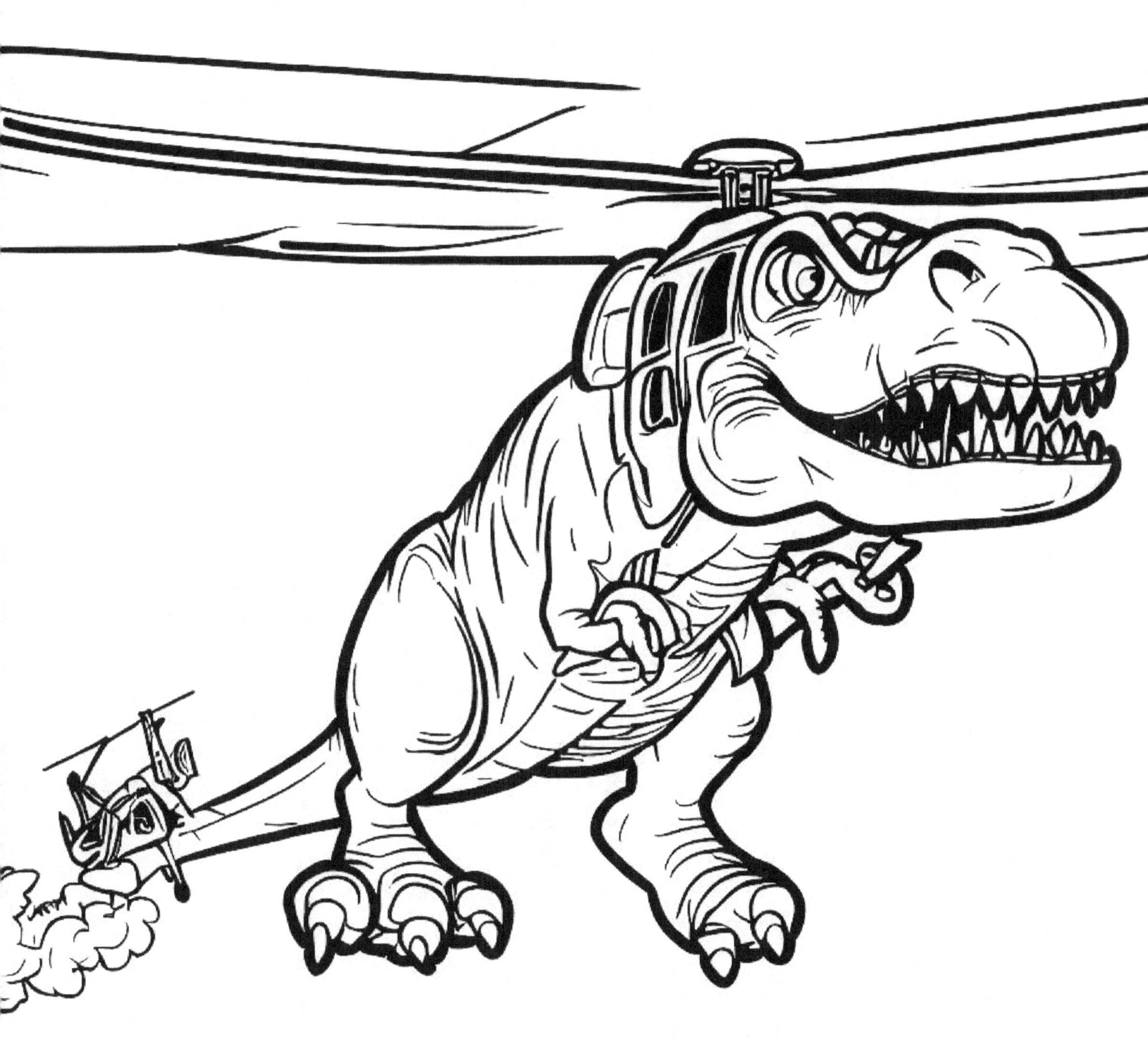

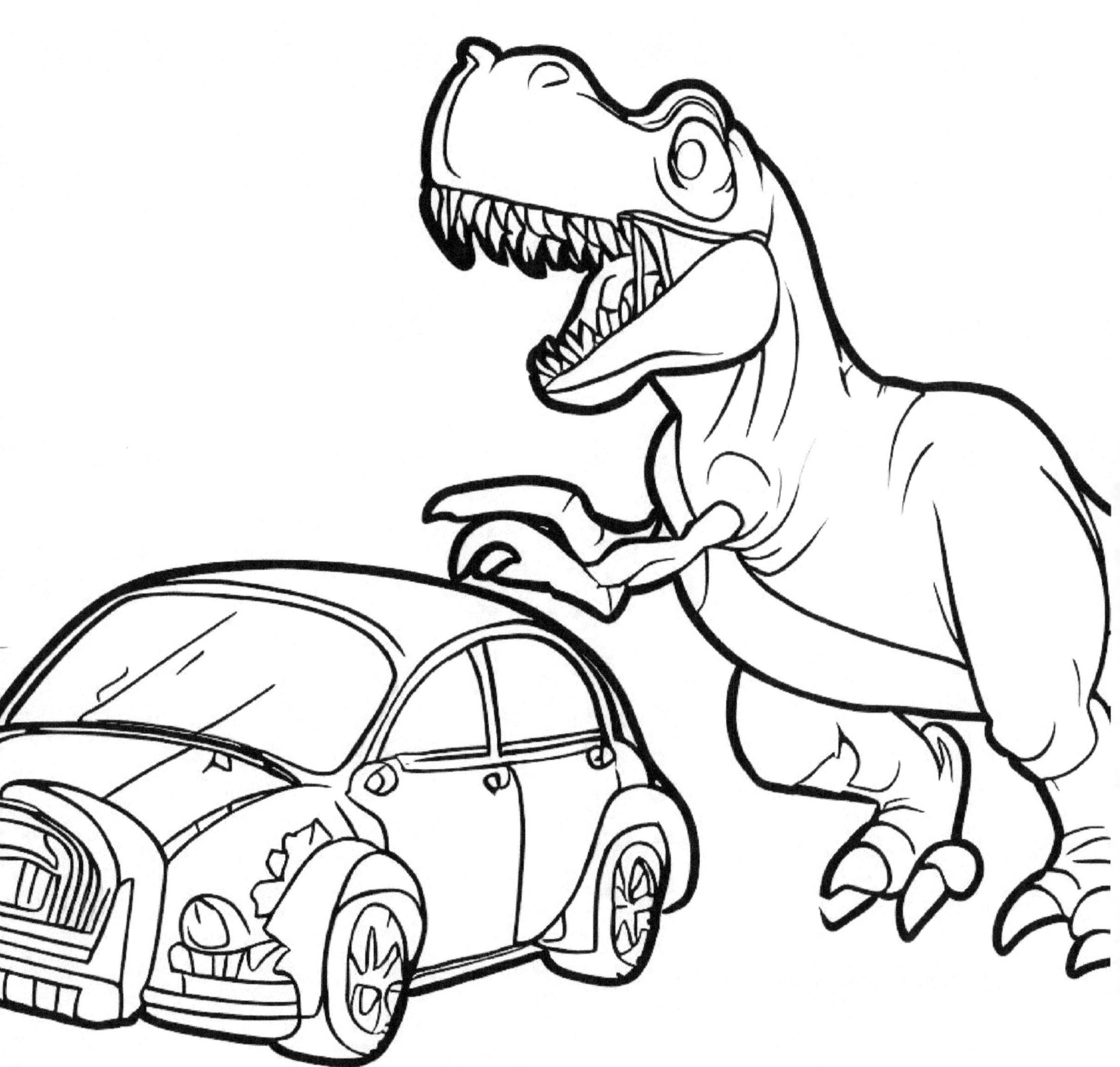

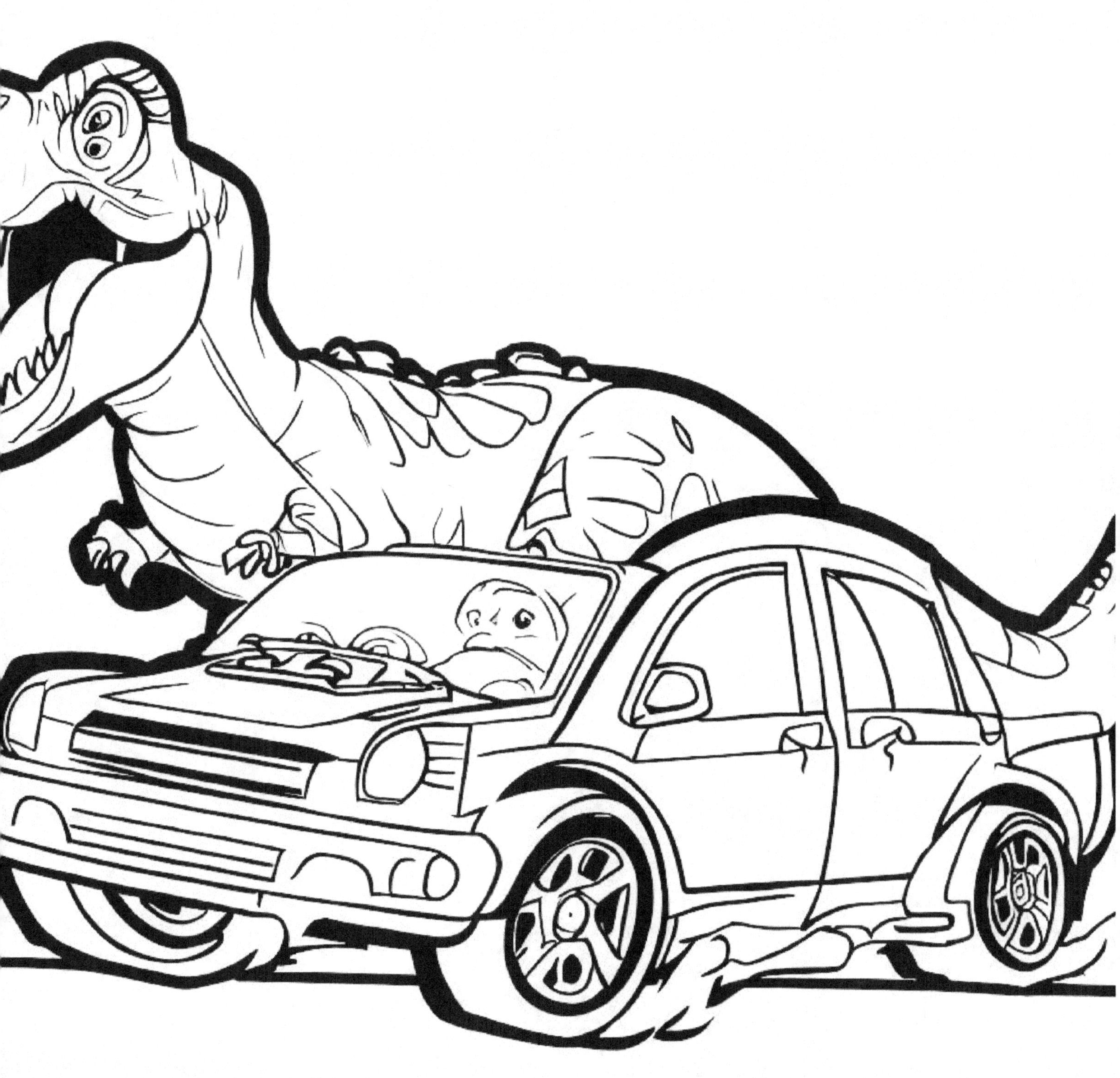

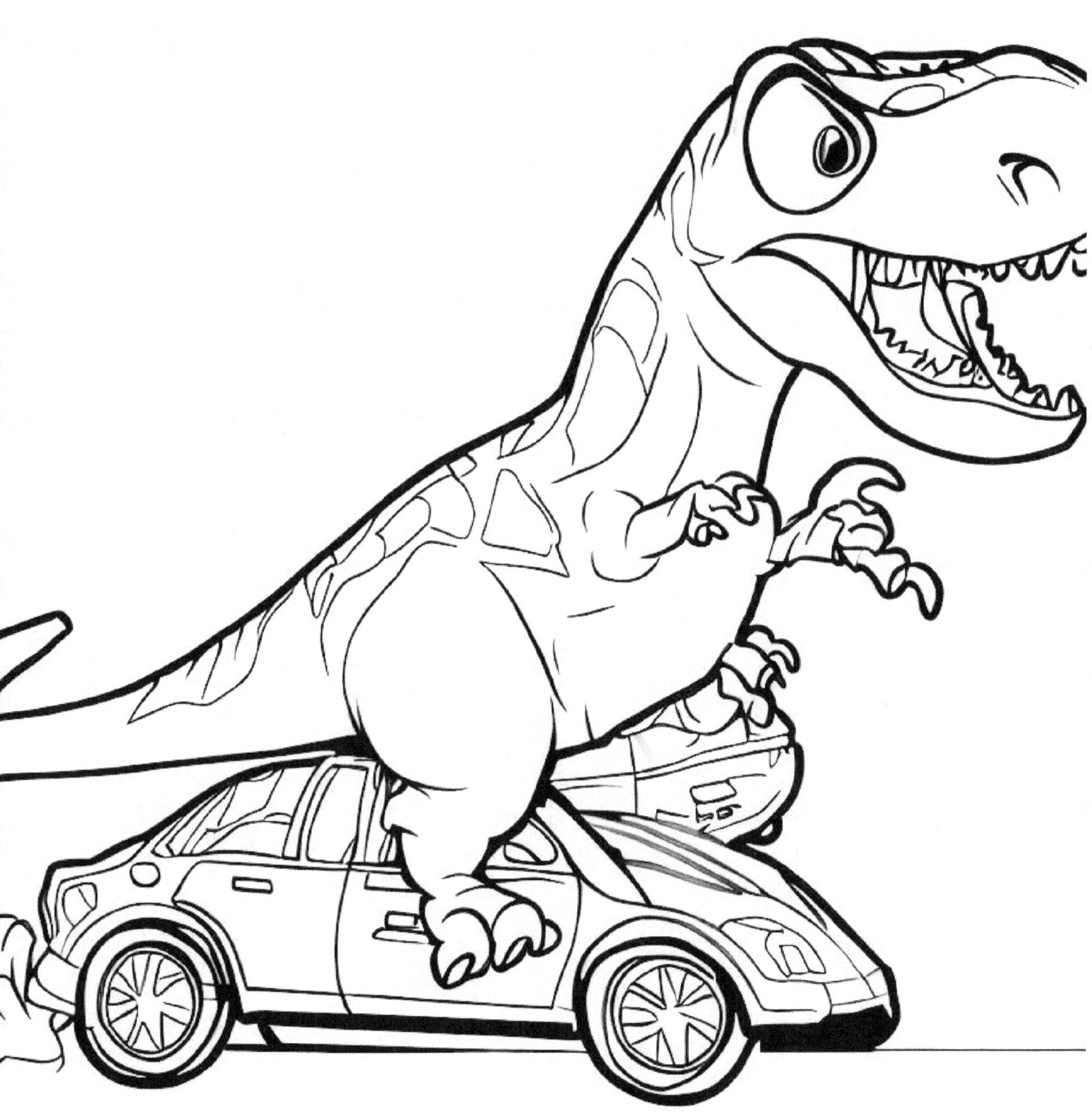

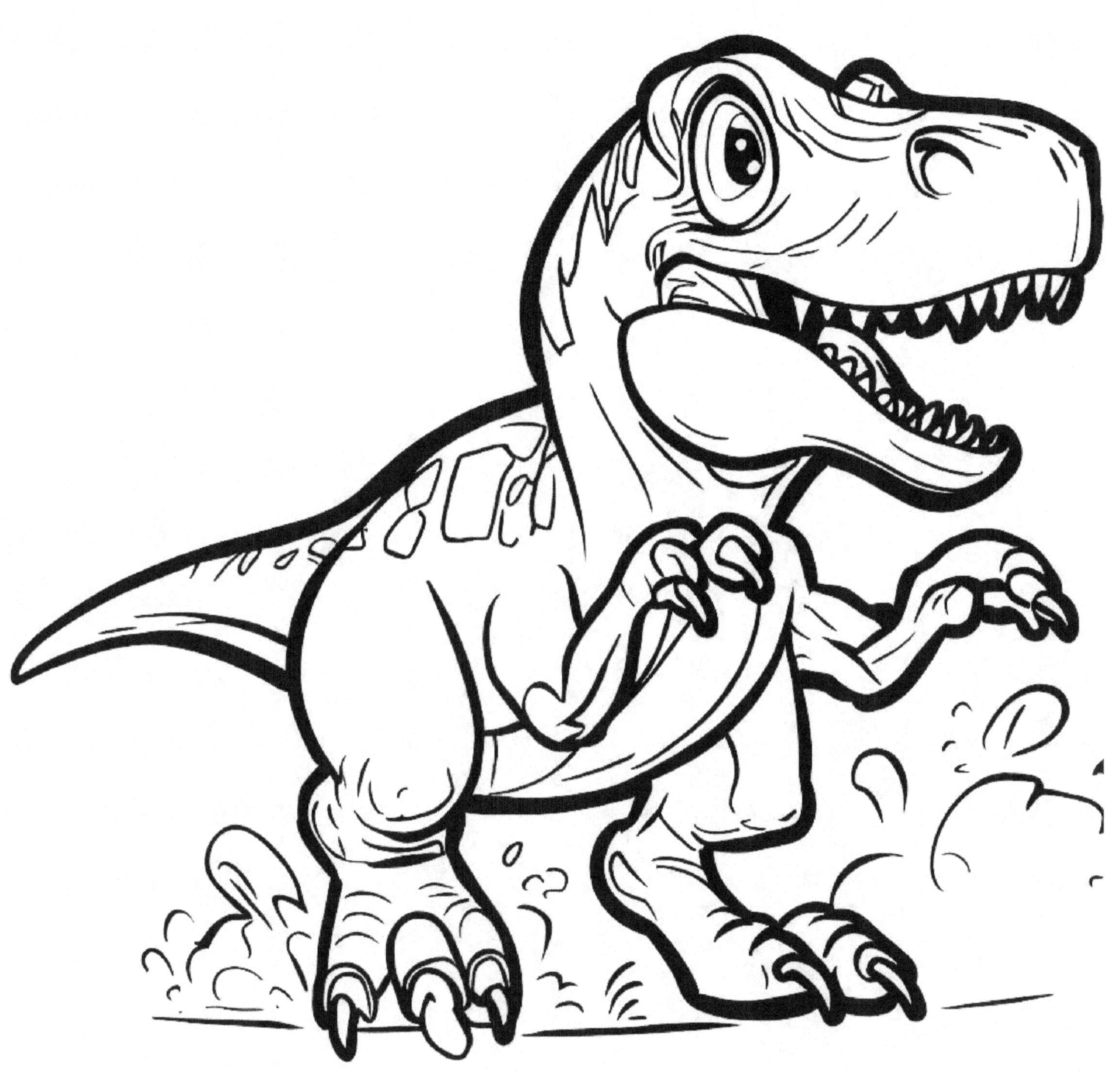

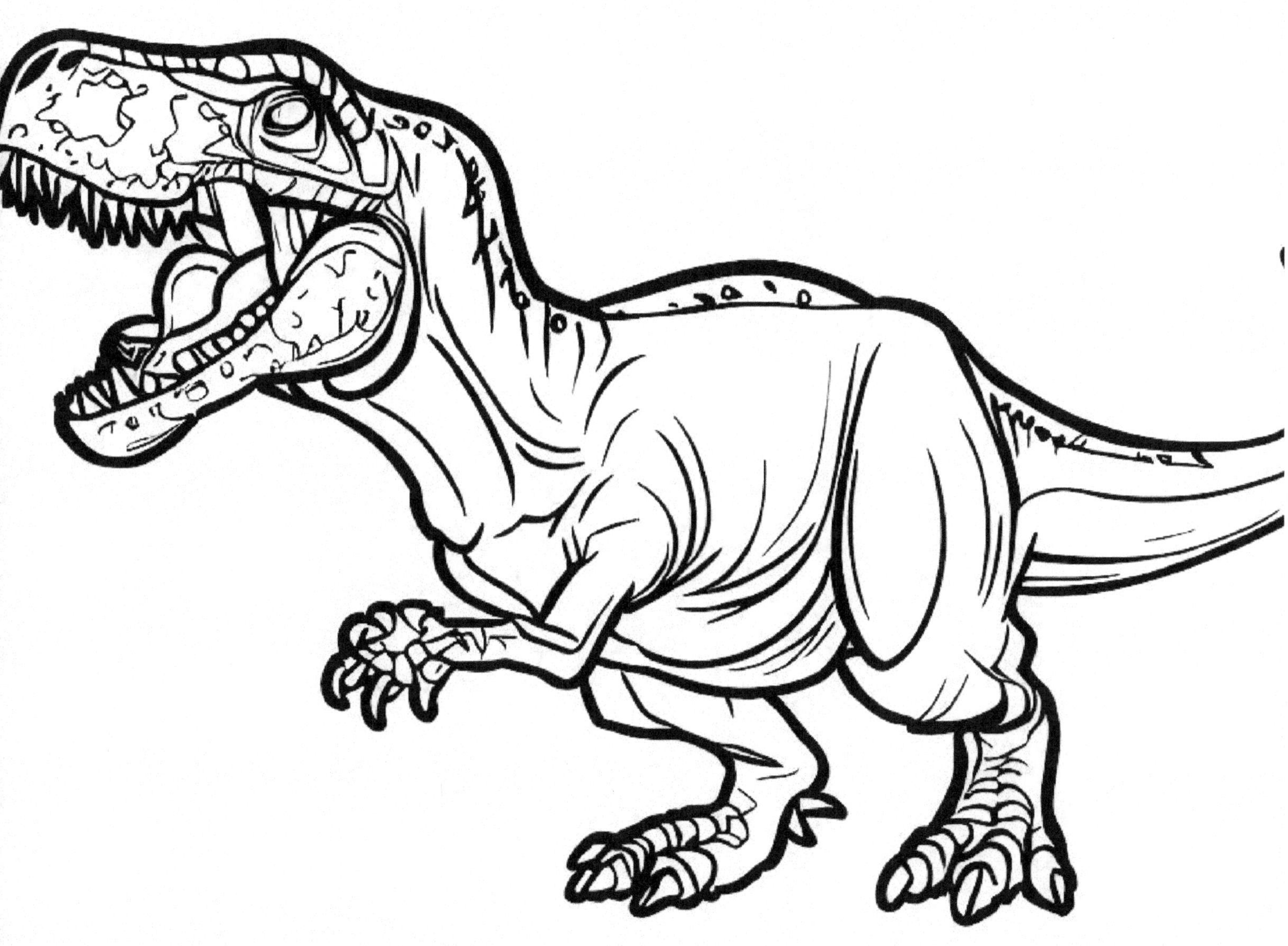

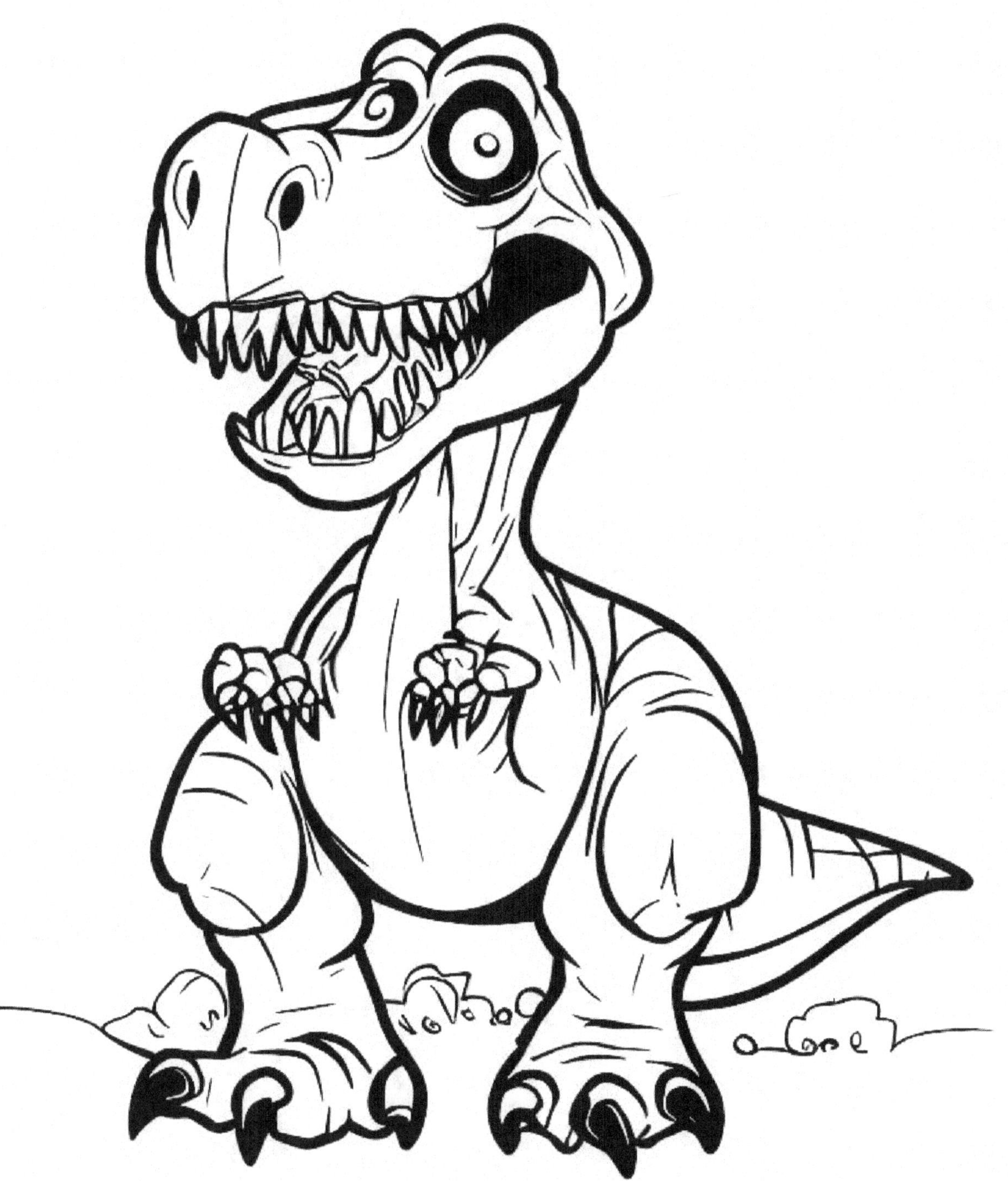

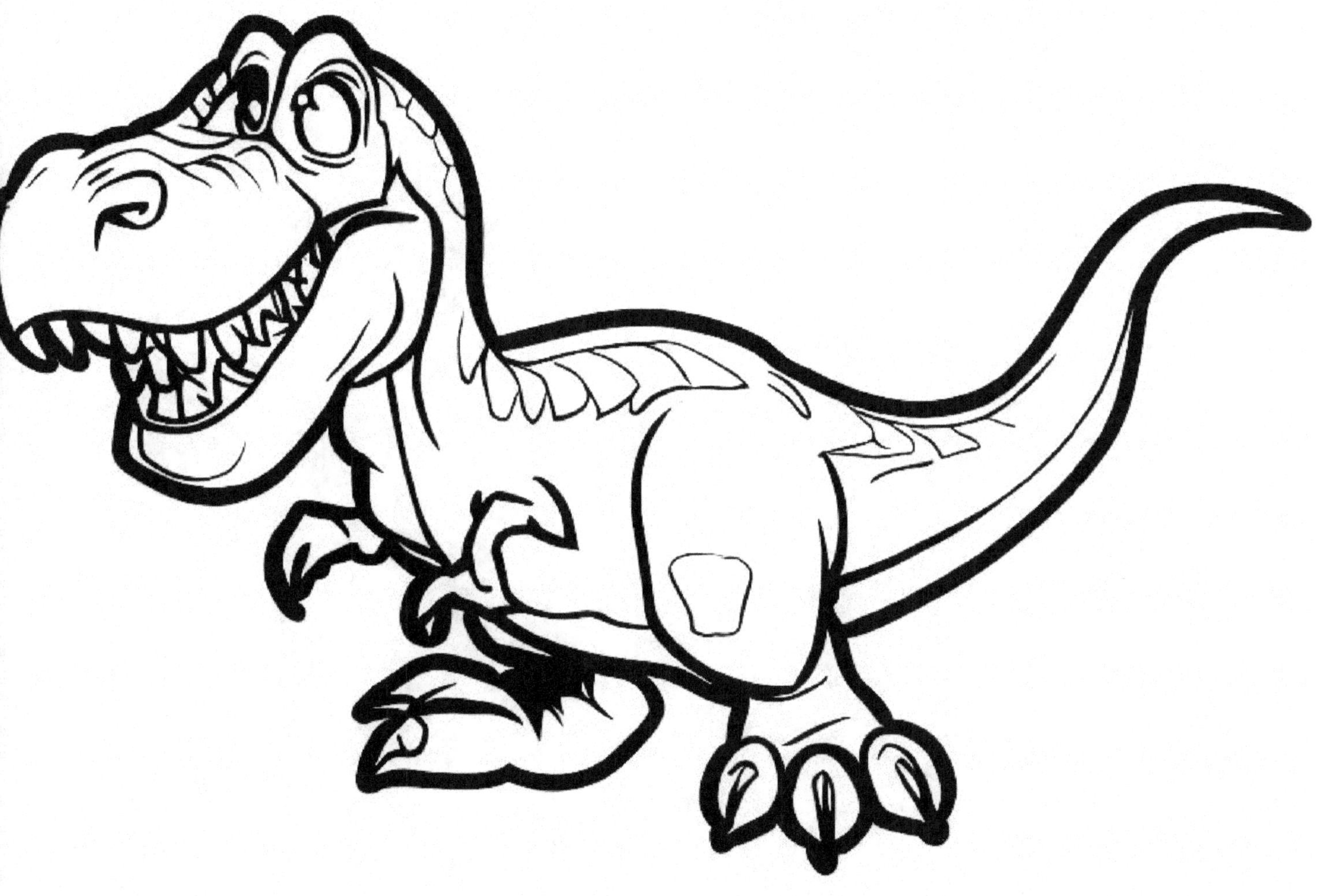

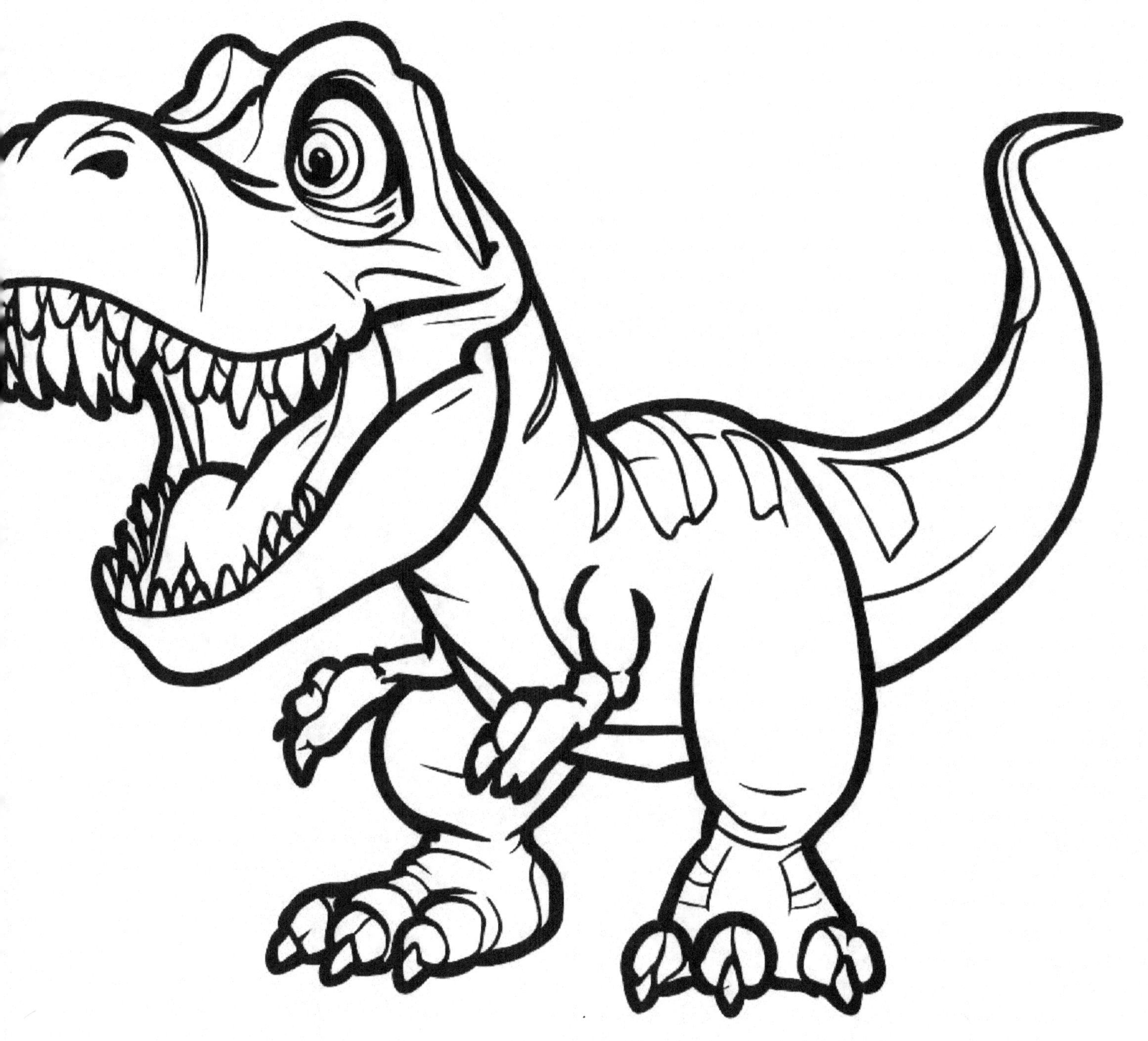

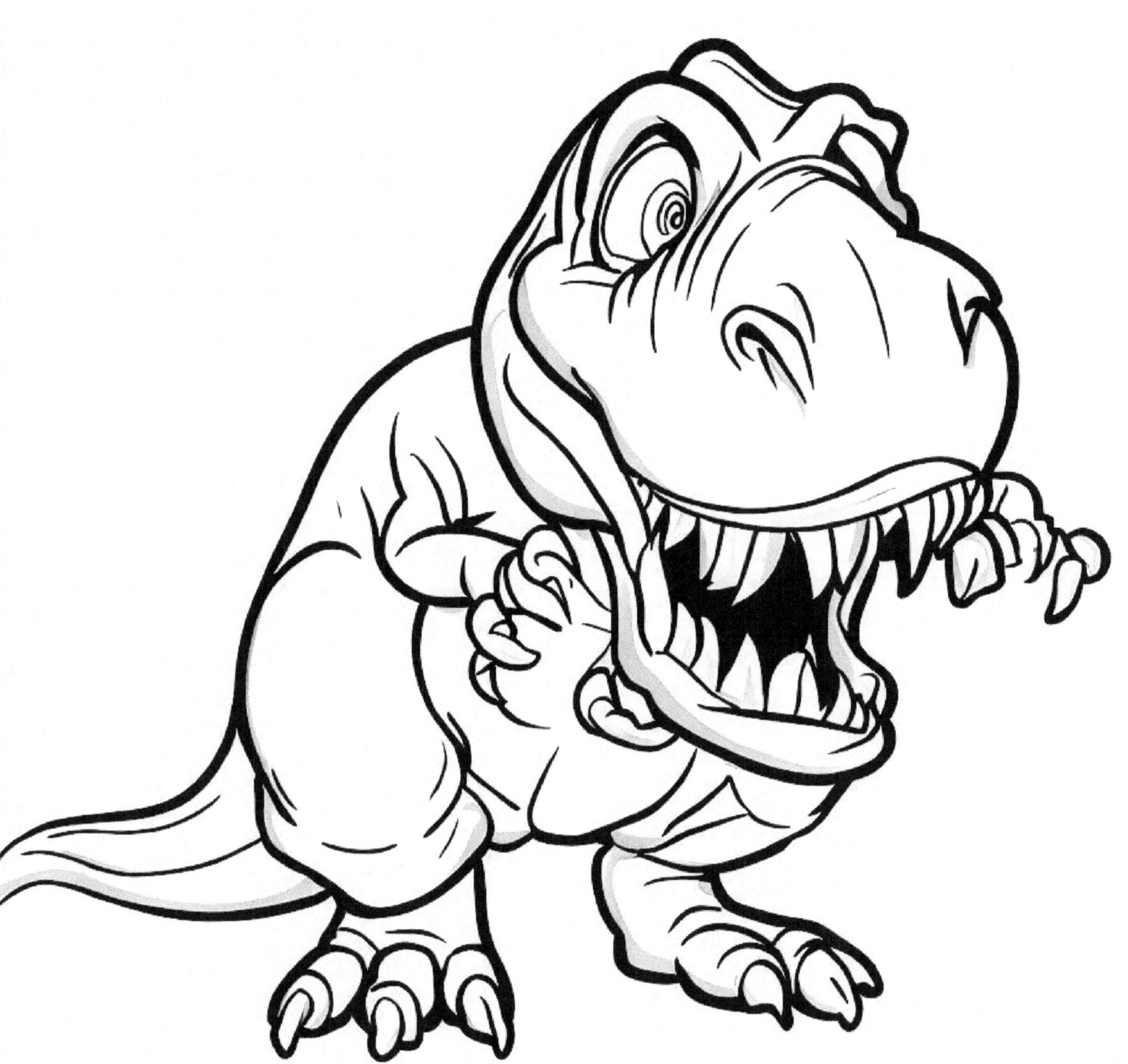

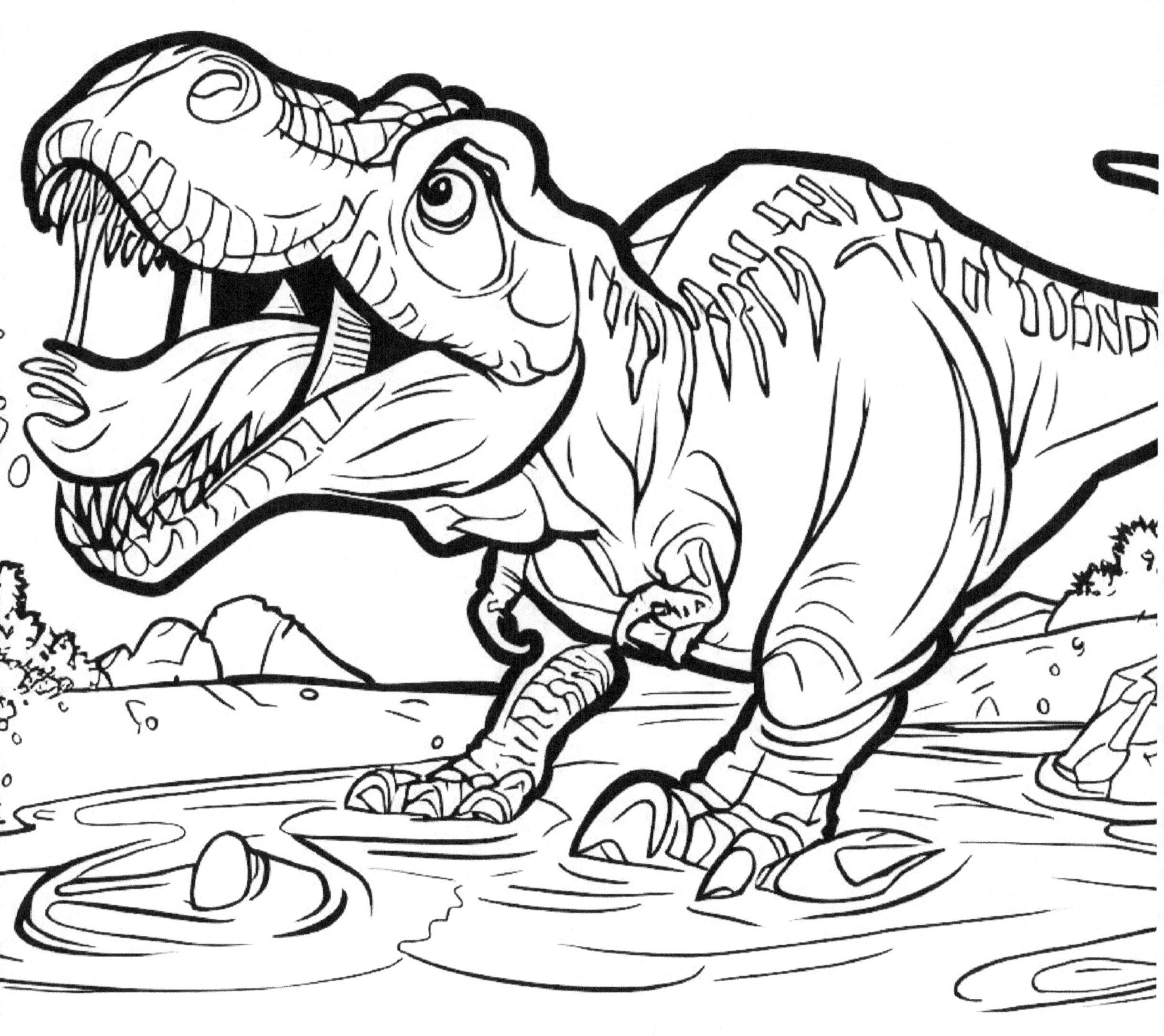

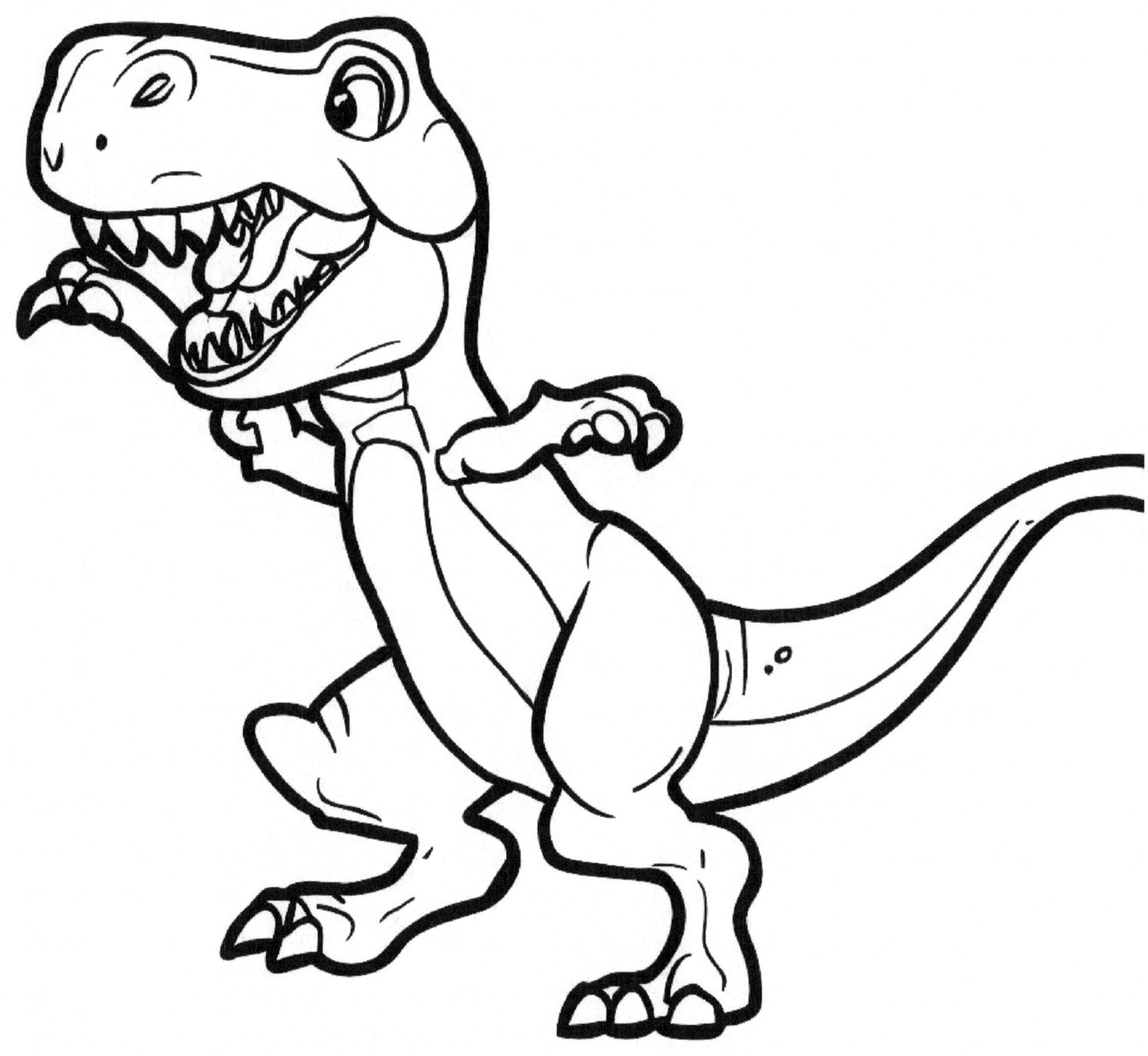

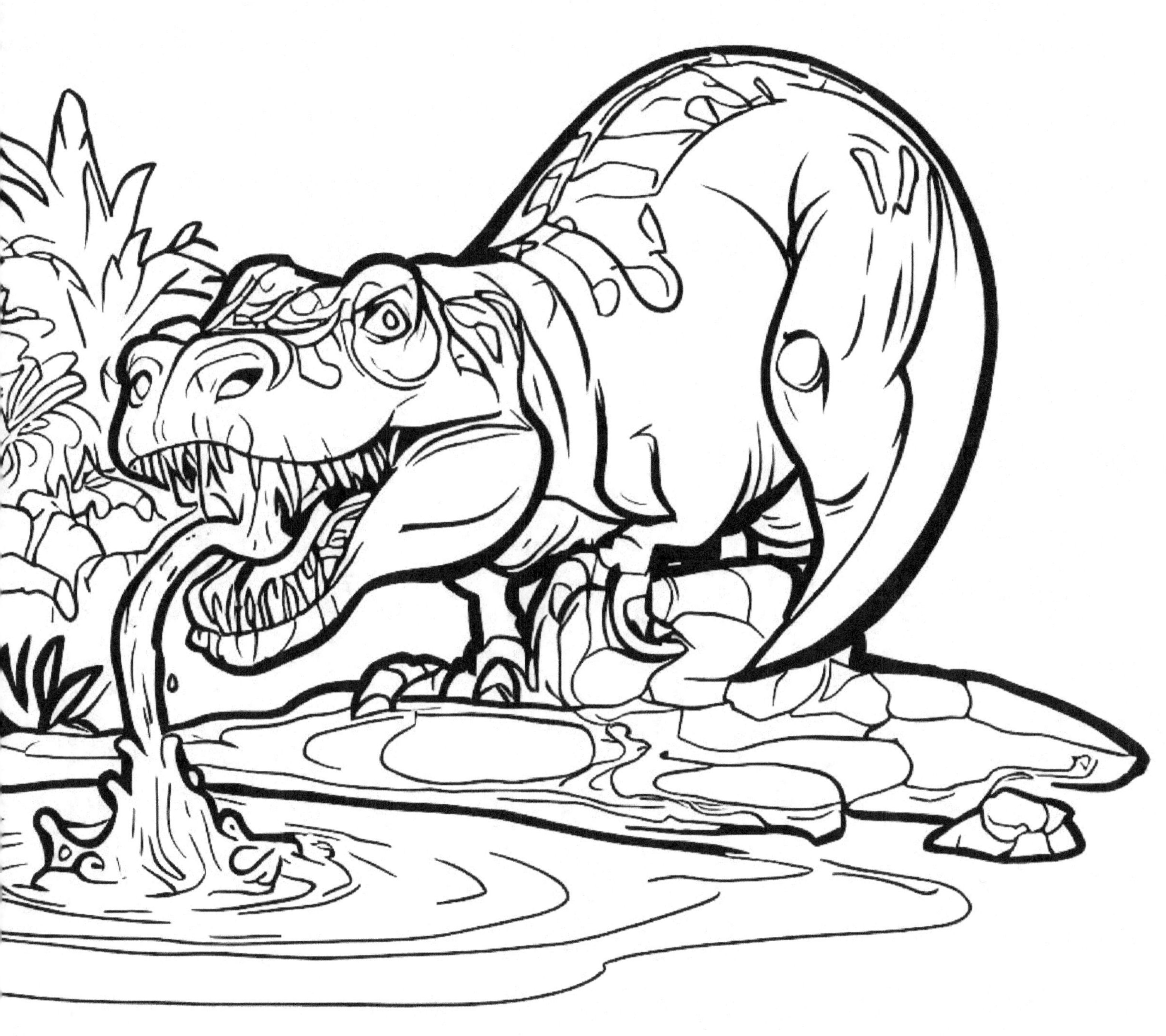

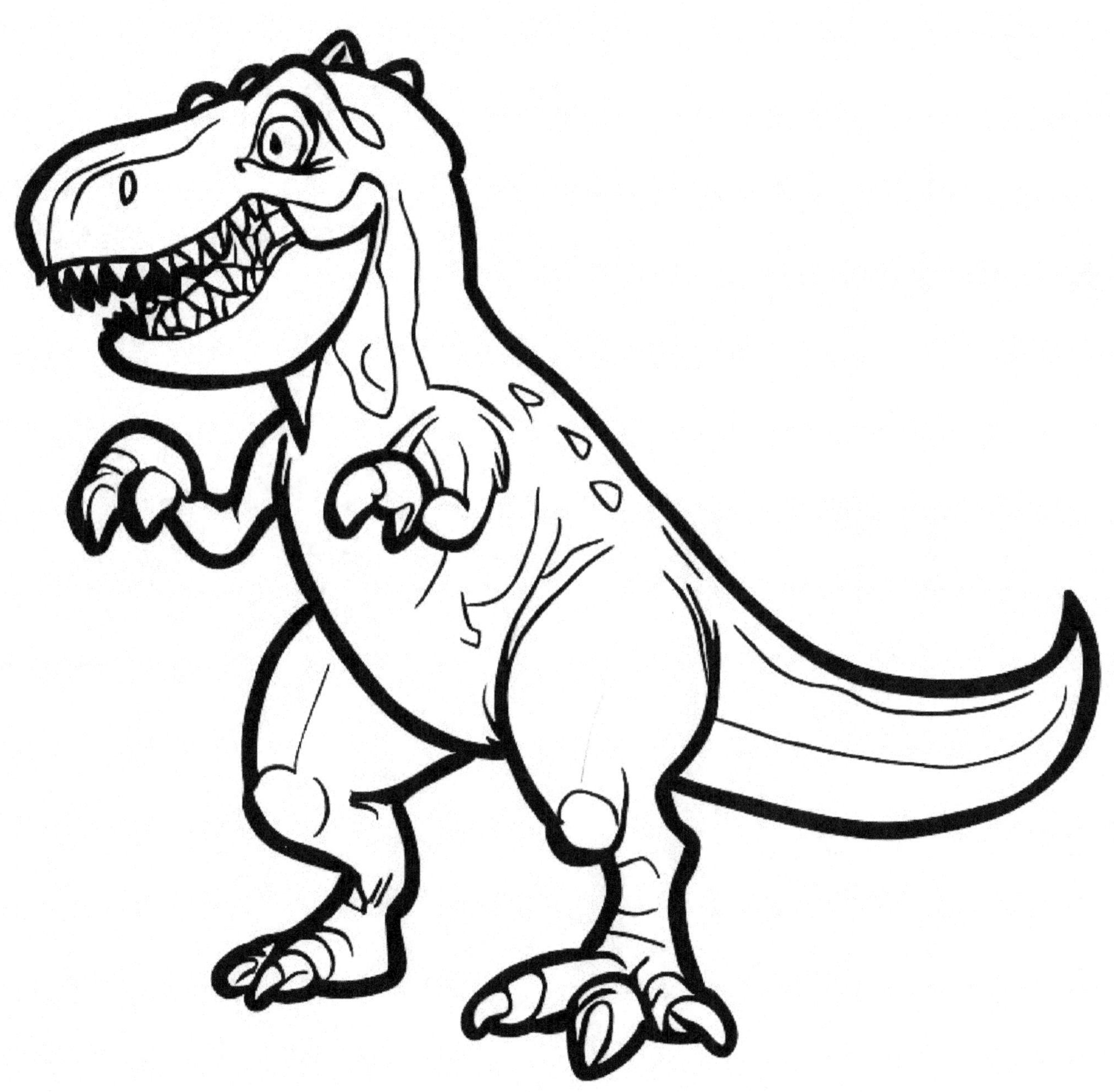

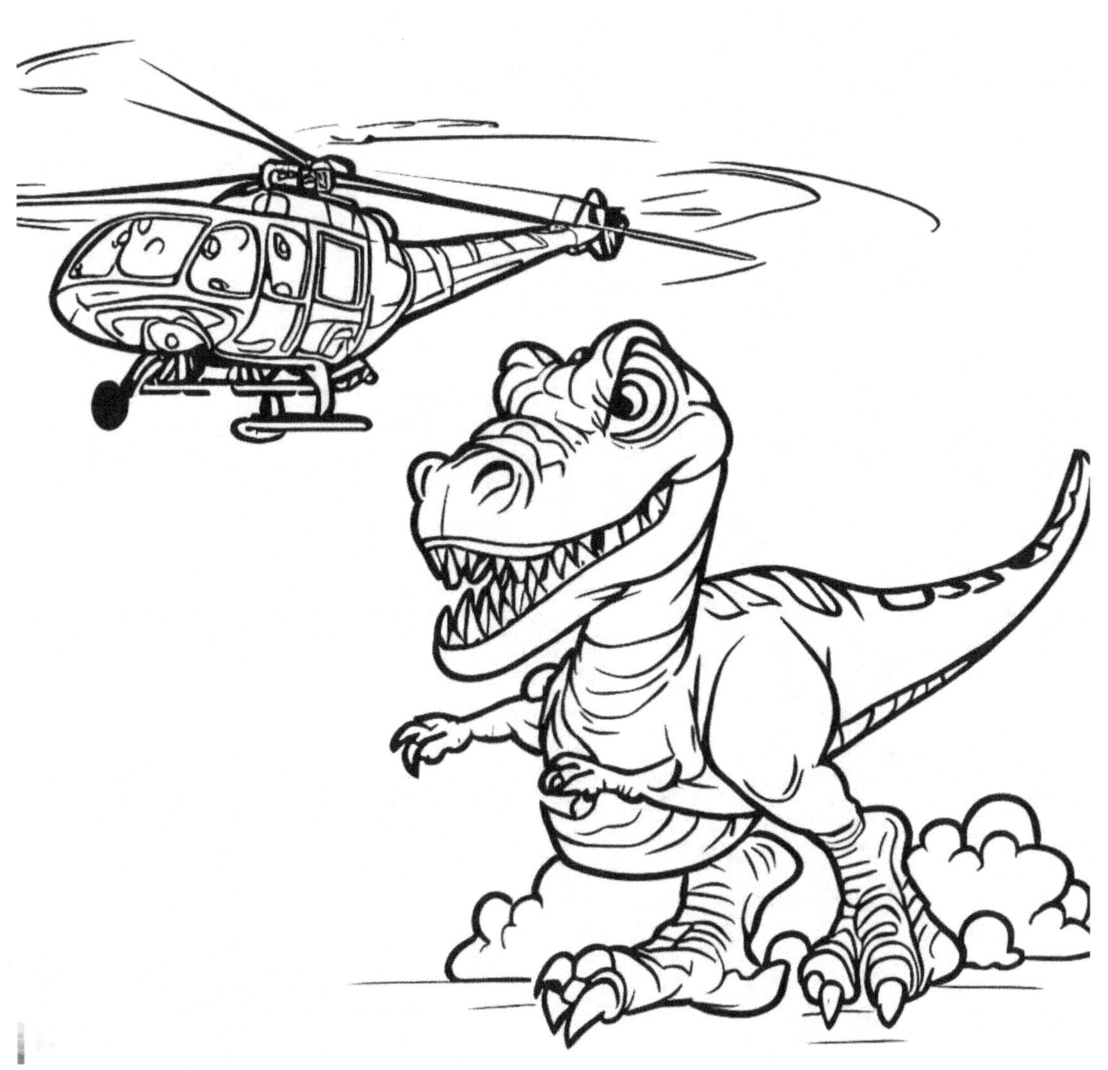

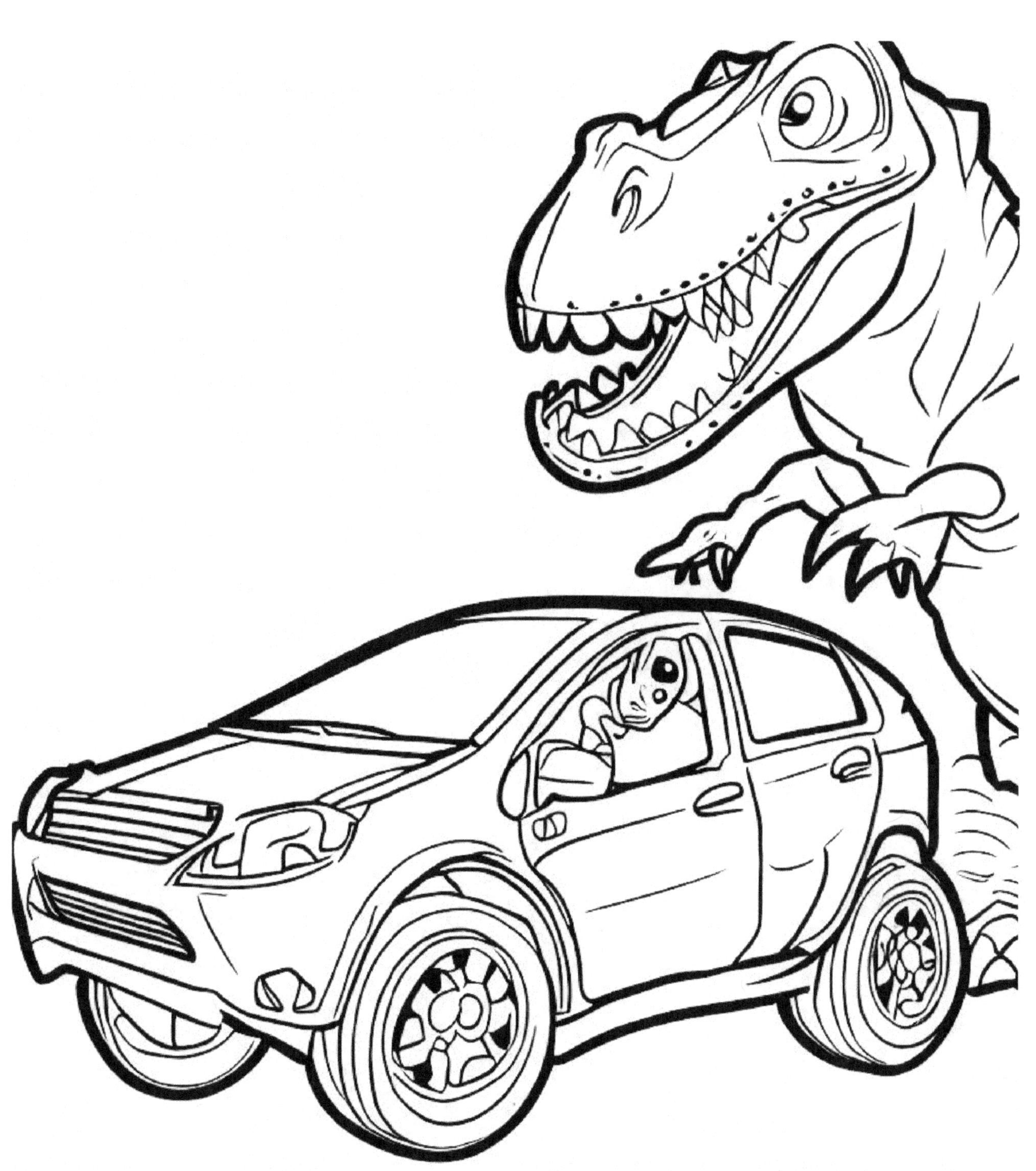

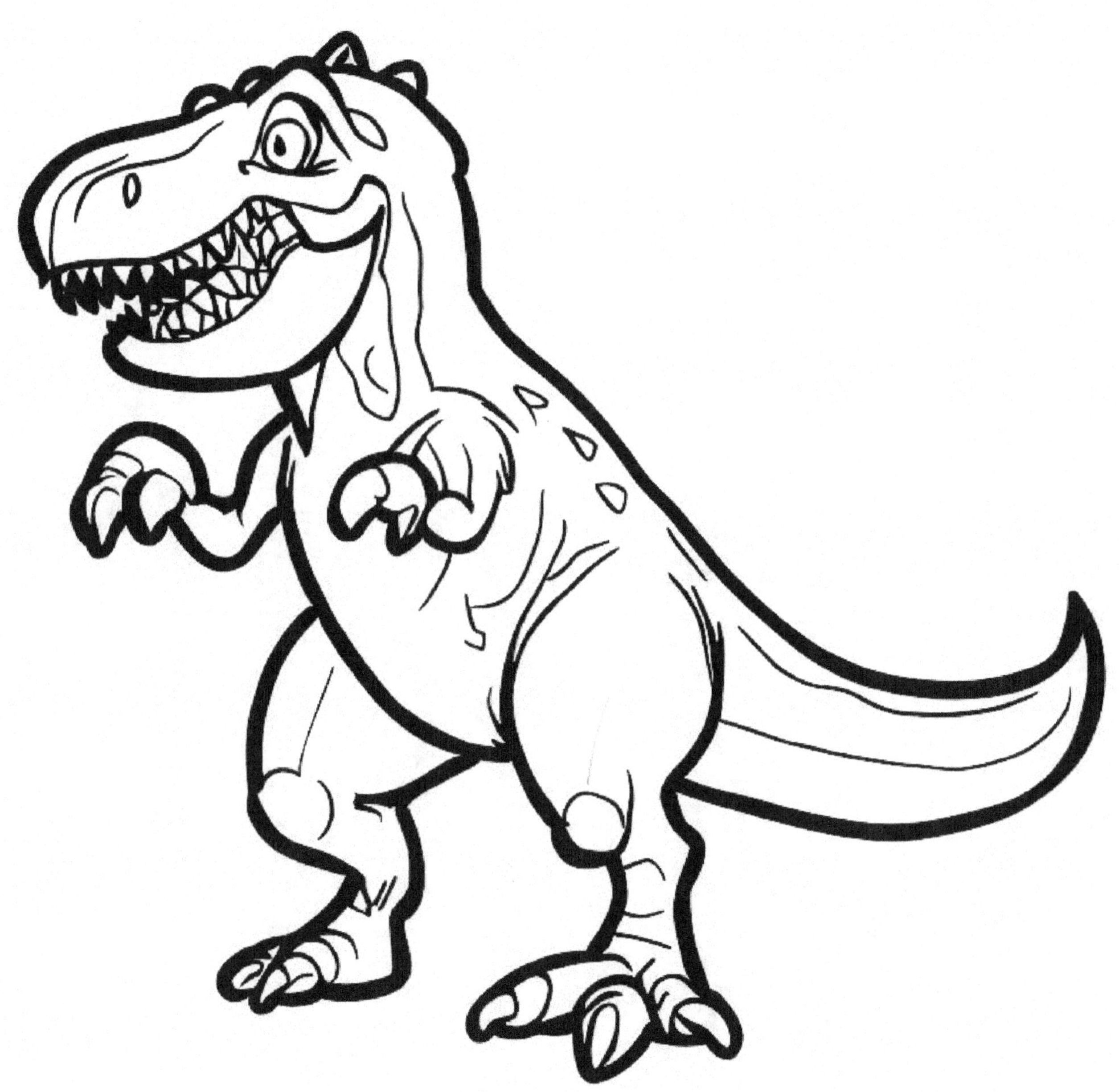

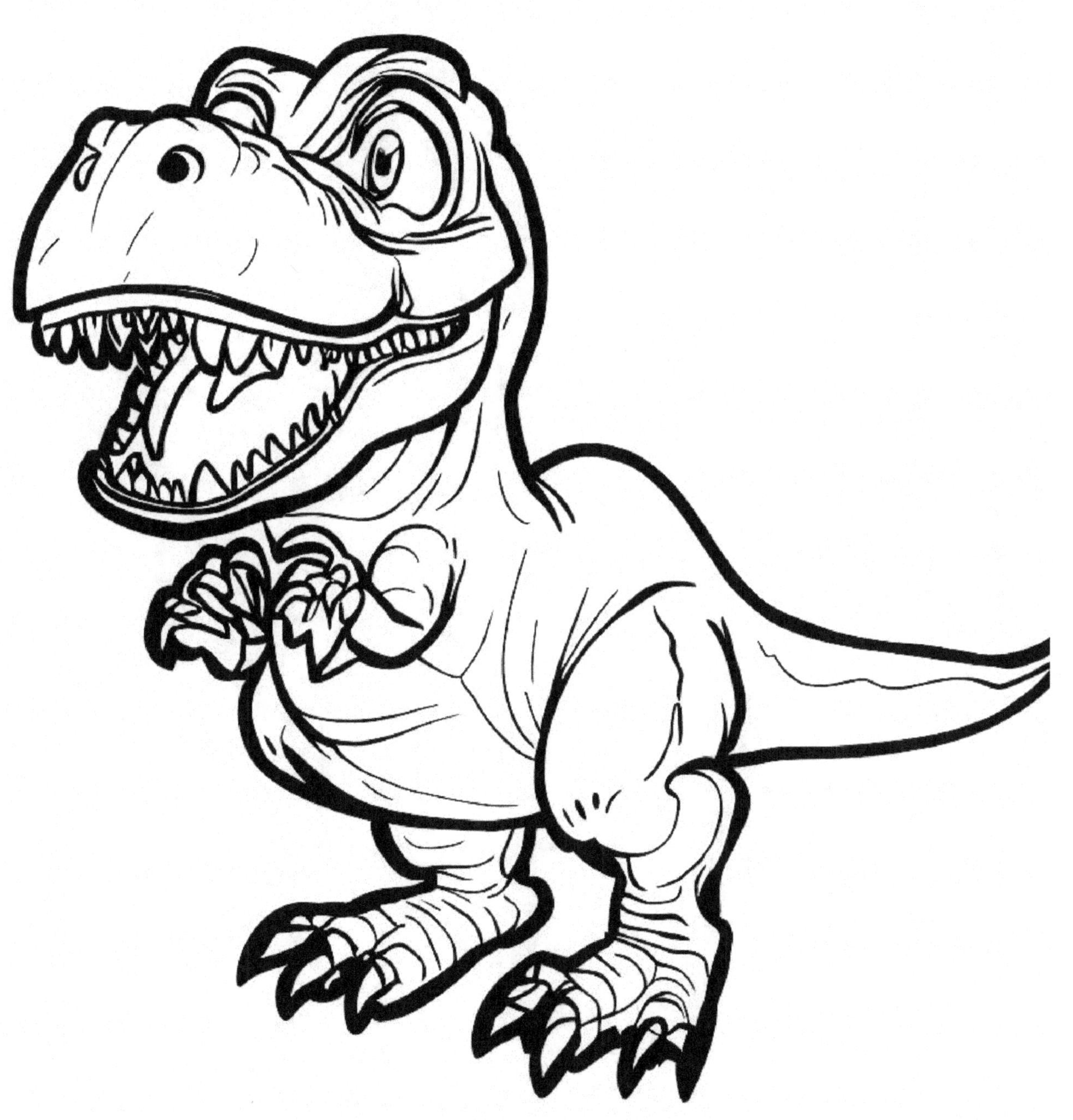

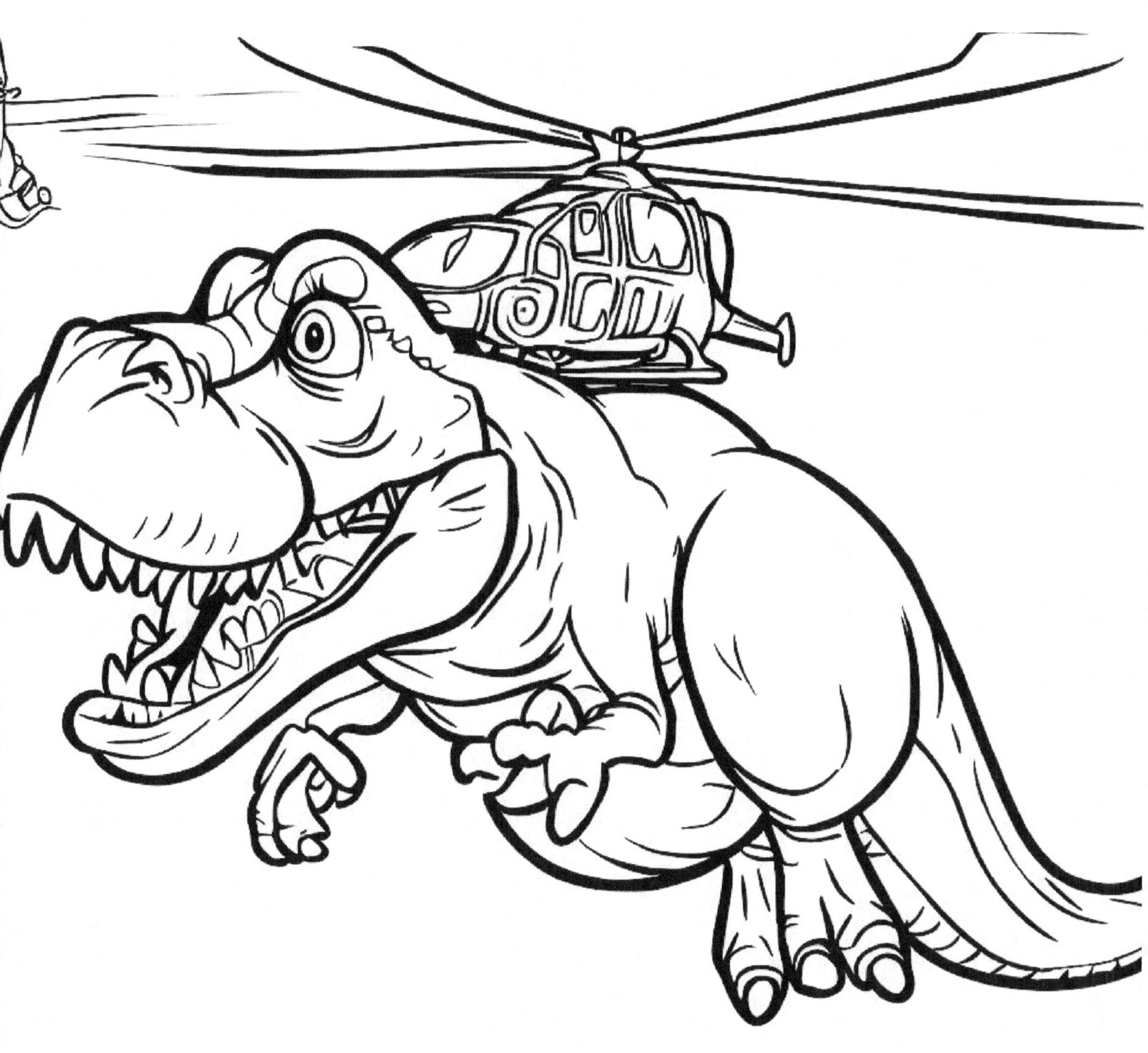

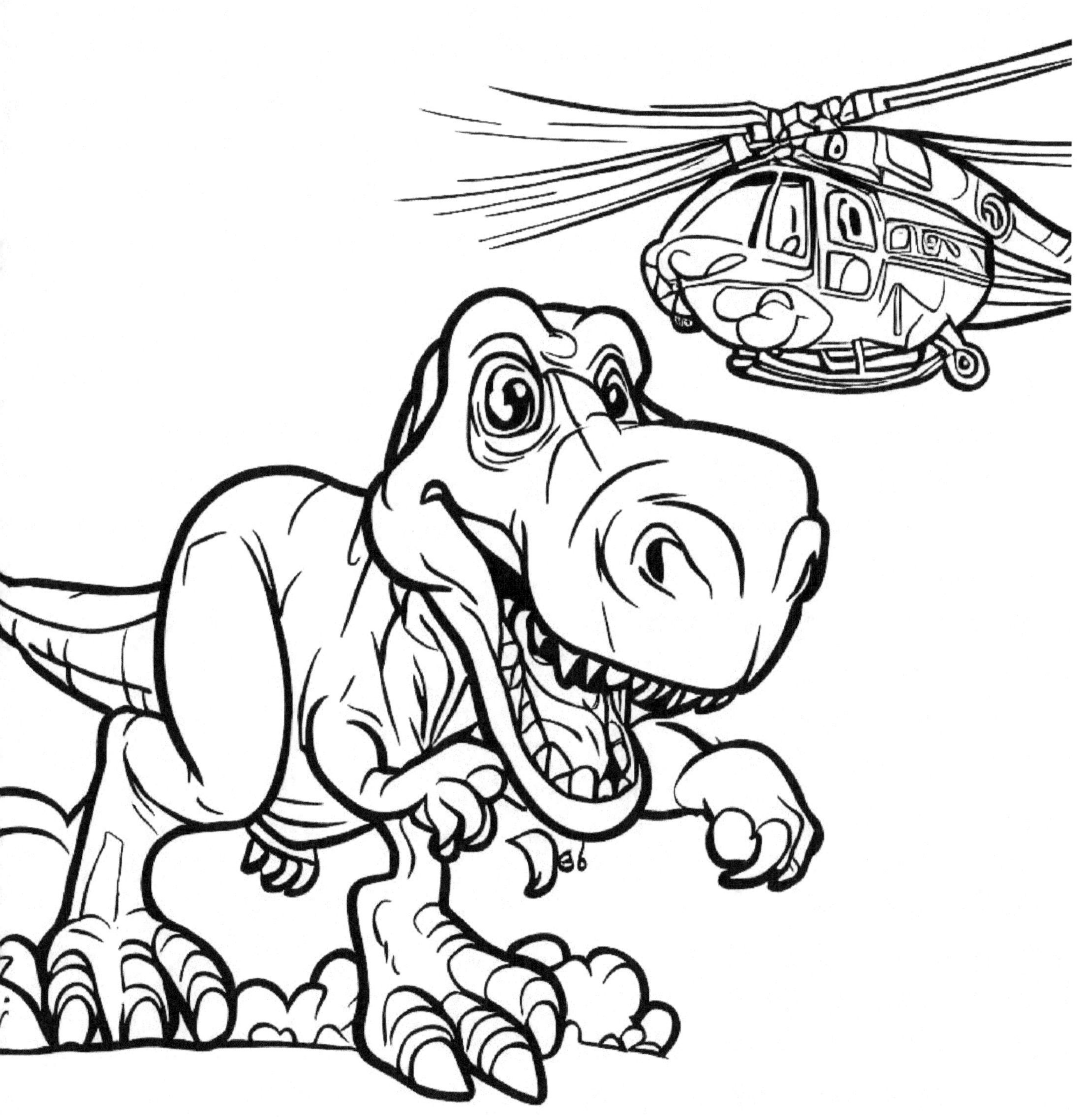

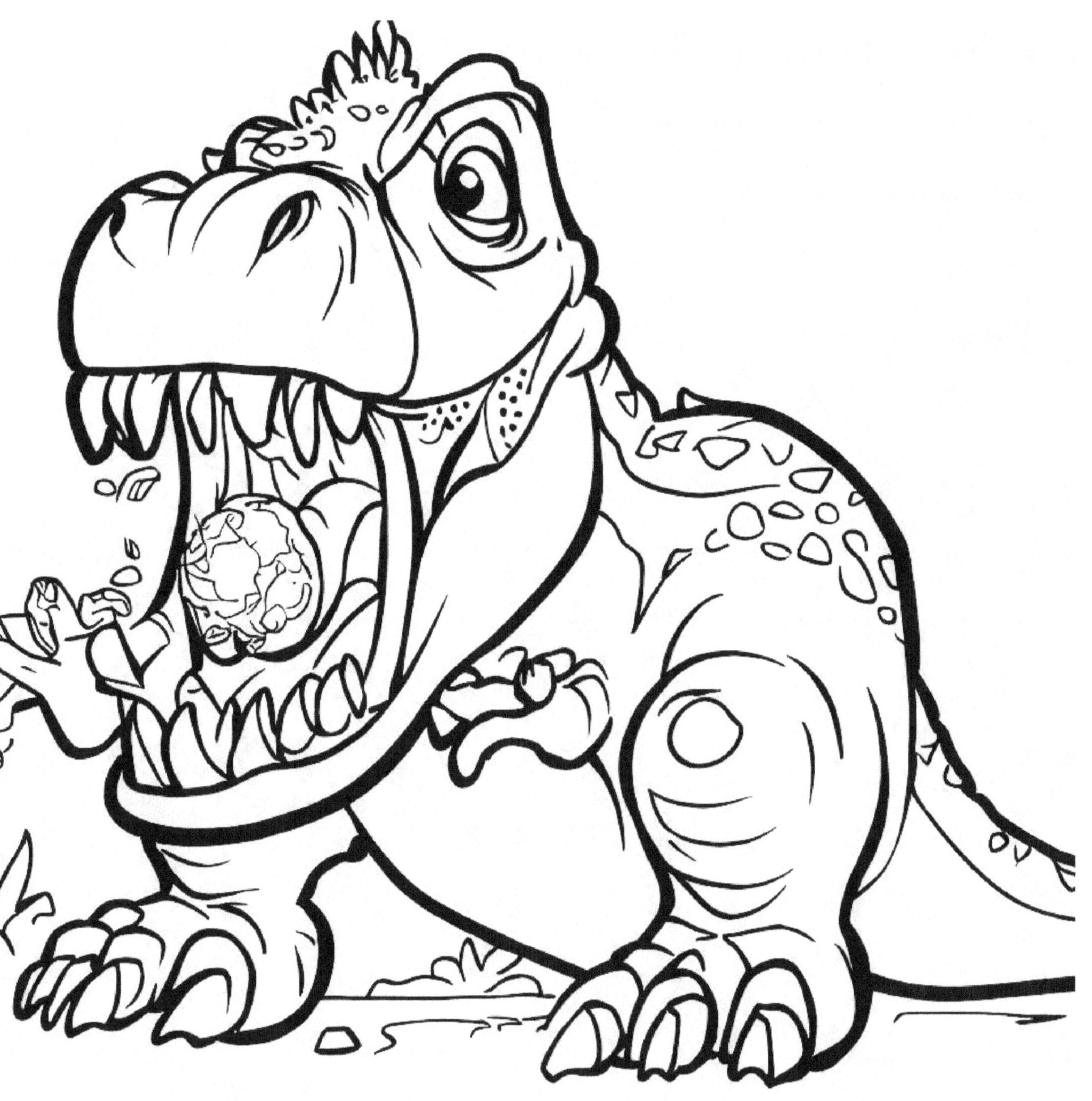

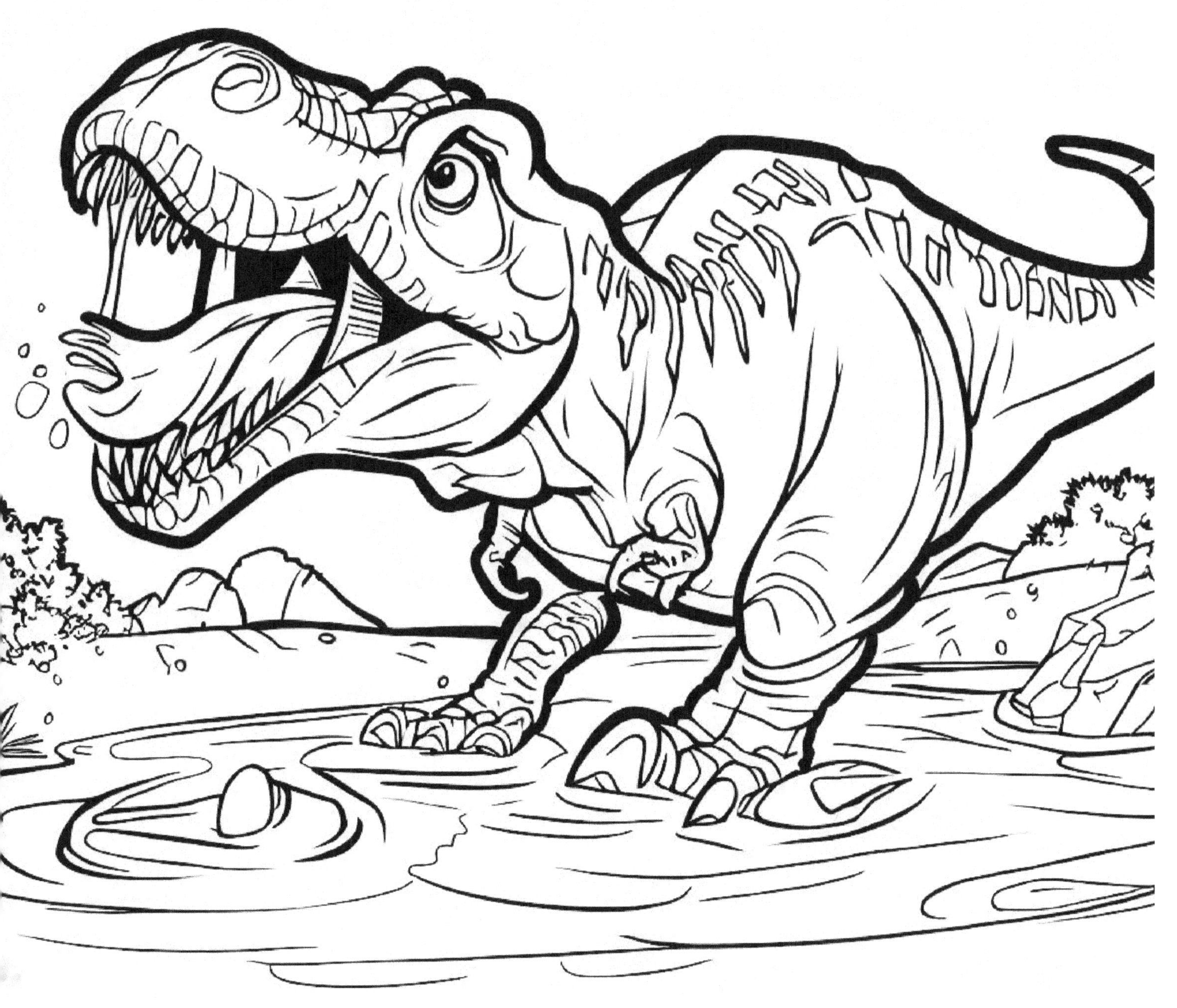

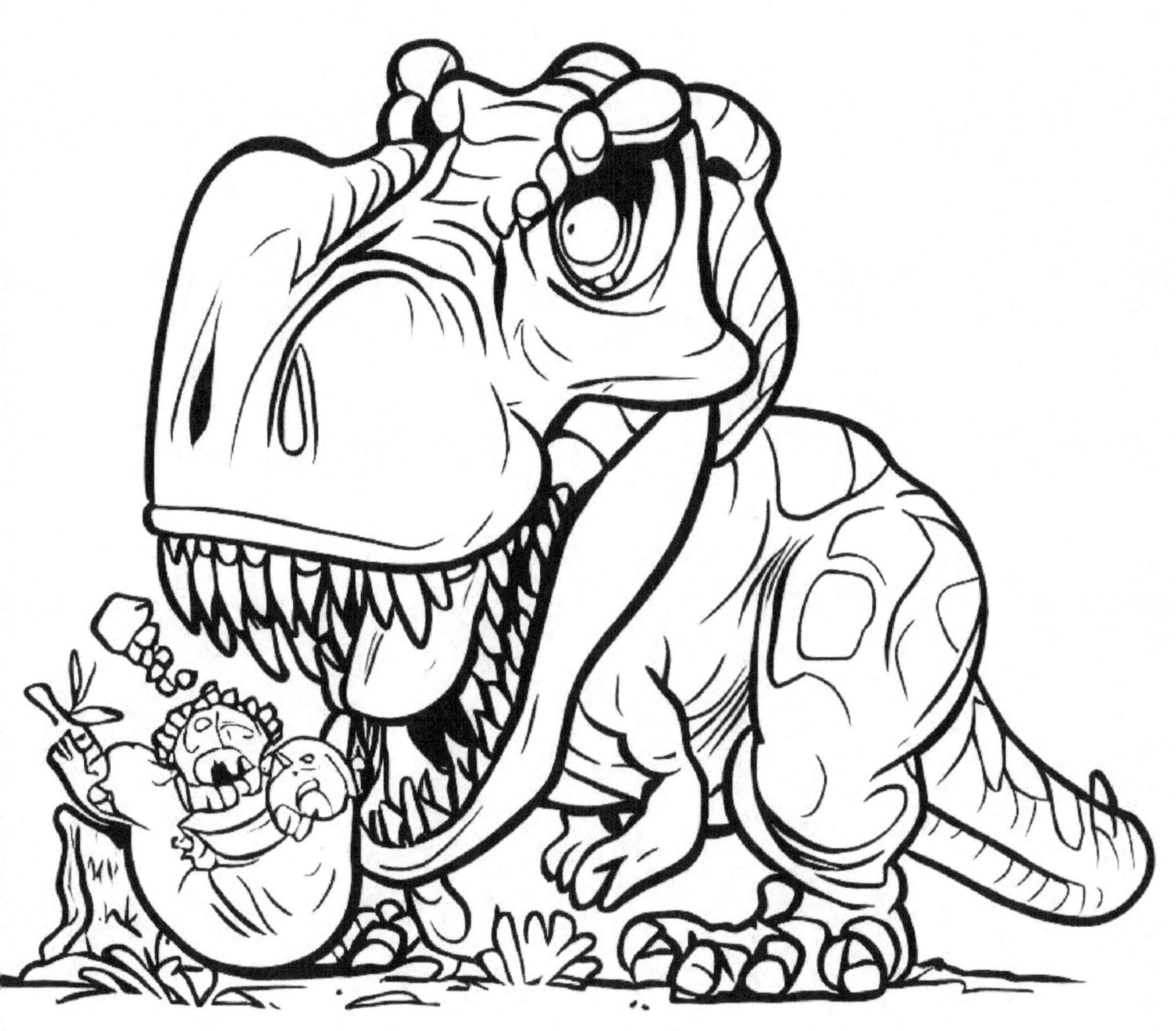

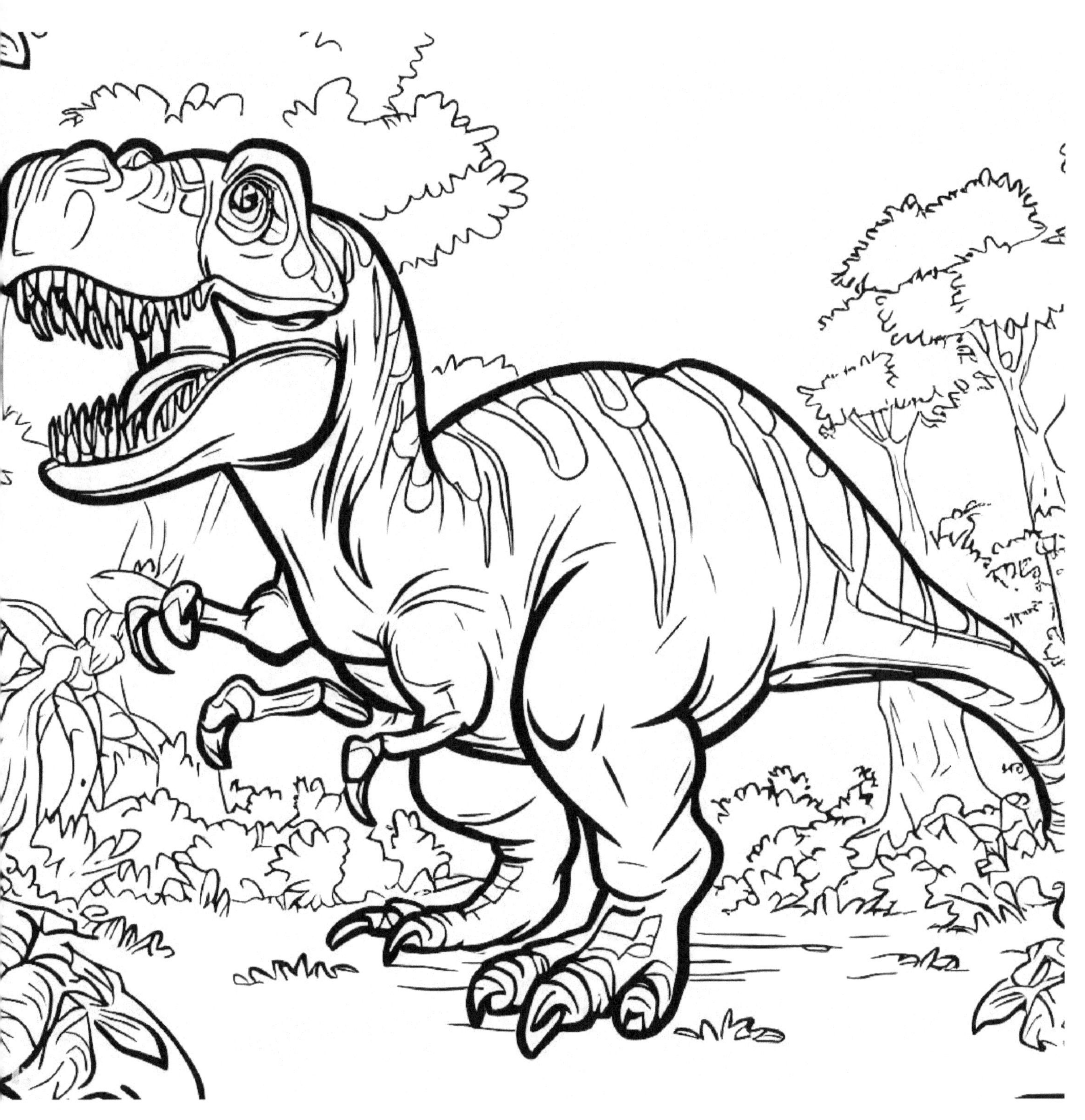

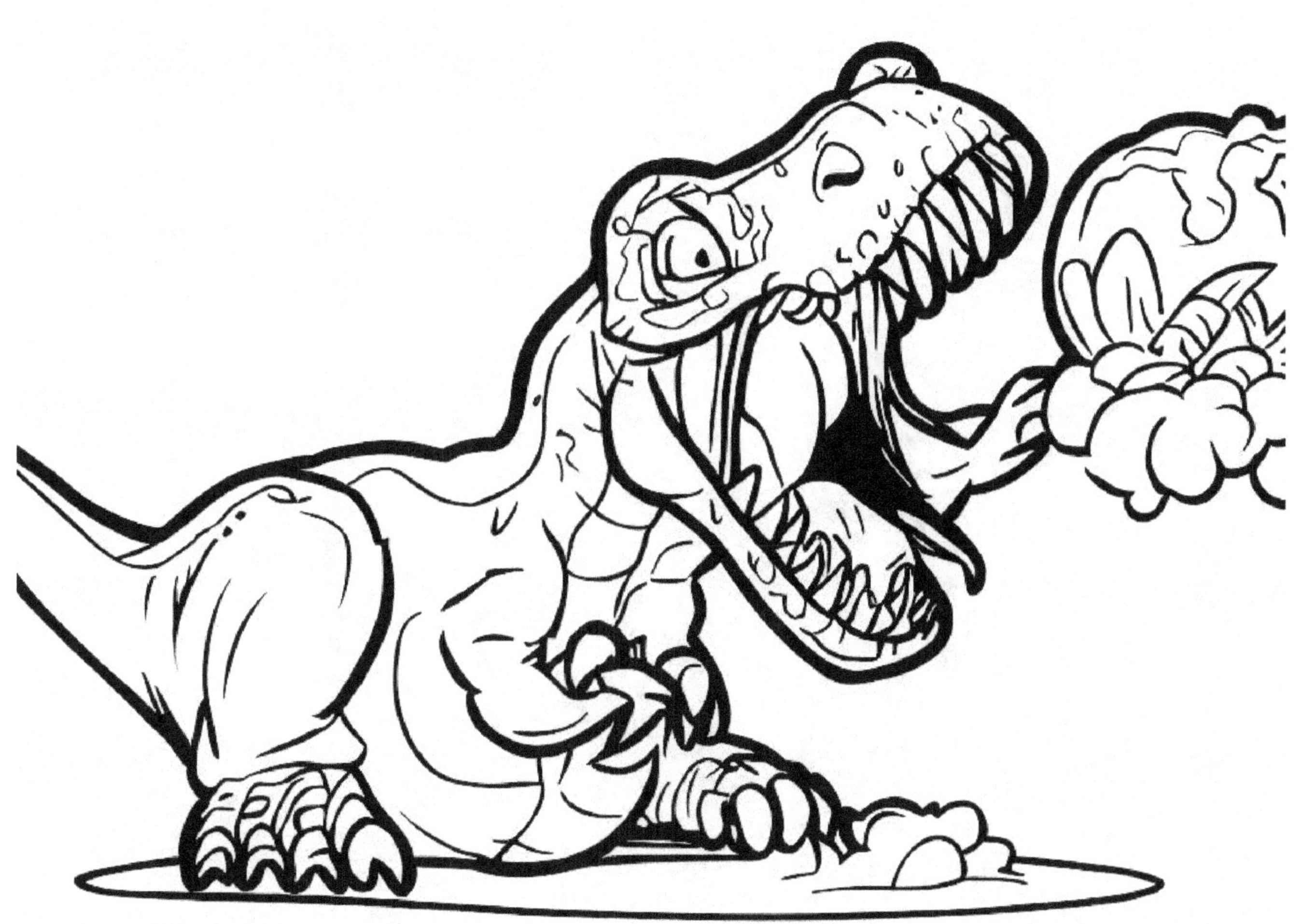